Children's
Bible Stories
for Bedtime

Children's Bible Stories for Bedtime

TO GROW IN FAITH & LOVE

Julie Lavender

Illustrated by Shahar Kober

Z KIDS • NEW YORK

ISBN: 9780593436165
Ebook ISBN: 9780593436158

Illustrations by Shahar Kober
Book design by Aimee Fleck

Printed in China

3 5 7 9 10 8 6 4

First Edition

To my grandson, Benaiah, and other
Lavender grand-treasures to come.

May you fall in love with God's Word
and delight in him daily.

Contents

New Testament 209

INTRODUCTION

Children's Bible Stories for Bedtime helps you connect with God before falling asleep. Reading God's Word just before bedtime reminds you that God is always with you—from morning until nighttime and even while you sleep.

The message of the stories leads up to and shares the gospel. God loved the world so much that he sent his Son, Jesus, to be the Savior. The good news of the gospel is that Jesus came to save people from their sins. Each story points to Jesus, from Old Testament to New, from the beginning to the end. Long before Jesus was born as a baby to Mary and Joseph, the stories reflect the need for a rescuer and God's promise to send one. God's promise comes true in the birth, life, death, and wondrous resurrection of Jesus.

These biblically accurate, faith-building stories, sprinkled with bright humor, encourage curious minds to think about the character of God and relish the warmth of his never-ending love.

At the end of each story, a time of brief Reflection helps you understand God's Word as it relates to you personally. The Prayer that follows leads you to speak openly and in confident relationship with the one who designed you, remains with you, and has a beautiful plan for your life.

Pondering these inspiring stories is the perfect, calming way to end the day and fall asleep in the comfort of God's presence and peace.

GETTING READY FOR BEDTIME

Winding down before bedtime helps your body get ready to fall asleep. A good night's rest is important for your body. It gives you the energy you'll need for another day of learning, playing, and drawing closer to God.

Here are 10 tips to help you settle down from the day and get ready for bed.

1. **Remove all screen activity at least one hour before bedtime.** Stay away from computers, televisions, phones, and other screens, and avoid playing video games. Games and screens excite the brain and prevent your body from getting sleepy.

2. **Take a bath and put on pajamas.** Be sure to hang the wet towel on a rack to dry. Brush your teeth, and be sure to put away the toothbrush and toothpaste.

3. **Tidy your room.** Put clothes, toys, books, shoes, and other items in their proper place. A cluttered room distracts the brain. A clean room calms the brain.

4. **Organize the clothes and supplies that you'll need for tomorrow.** Choose the outfit you want to wear to school, church, or playtime. Find the matching shoes. Set out a jacket, sweater, or raincoat, if needed. Make

sure school supplies, sports equipment, dance shoes, or other extracurricular items are handy. Place everything in one location.

5. **Get one last drink of water.** Be sure to put the dirty glass away.

6. **If it's not quite time for bed yet, listen to calming music.** Or think of something happy and positive, and then draw it in a picture.

7. **Talk with a parent or guardian about good things that happened today, and make a list of God's blessings.** You could even keep a journal by your bed to write in each night. Think of all the things you can be grateful for!

8. **Give family members a bedtime hug.**

9. **Read a Bible story with an adult or on your own.**

10. **Say prayers.** Talk to God, and be sure to thank him for taking such good care of you and for loving you with a never-ending love. Ask God to take care of your family and friends, as well as the whole world. Tell God your concerns too. Finally, ask God to give you a good night's rest.

PART ONE

Old Testament

God Creates the World

GENESIS 1

A long, long time ago, the planet was dark and empty. A big bunch of water covered it, but there was nothing else. Except for God.

And then God *created*—he turned the planet into a magnificent world.

God is so powerful and mighty and holy that his very words spoke the heavens and *everything* on earth into being. And he did it in just six days.

On the first day of creation, God said, "Let there be light." And, POOF! Just like that, there was light! Everywhere! It's like flipping your bedroom light switch to turn the lights on. Only, God spoke the words, "Let there be light," and the whole ginormous universe became filled with light.

Then God separated the light and the darkness. He called the light "day," and he called the darkness "night." That was day one.

On day two of God's creation, God said, "Let there be space between the waters." As soon as he said it, some of the water lifted from earth. It rose up, up, up, and then it stayed high above, all around the planet. This left a space in between the waters. God called the space "sky." So, on day two, God created sky.

On the third day of creation, God said, "Let all the water under the sky come together, and let dry ground appear." And, once again, POOF! All the water whooshed here and there to form ponds and lakes and oceans. Where water had once been, dry ground now sat. Some flat ground. Some hilly ground. Huge mountains too.

But he didn't stop there. Day three was a big one! God also created trees—so many that they filled the earth. Willow trees, pine trees, palm trees . . . He created so many trees, we don't have time to name them all!

But God still wasn't done. He covered the ground with bright green grass. Flowers popped out on the earth in all colors and shapes. He created sunflowers, tulips, lilies, roses, and lots more.

Garden vegetation sprang up too, like corn, green beans, tomatoes, potatoes, pumpkins, peppers, and peas. (By the way, which vegetables do you kind of wish God might *not* have created? Carrots? Broccoli? Squash?) Also on day three, God created fruit trees and every other kind of plant that grows fruit.

God created all those things—lakes, dry ground, trees, plants, and flowers—on day three.

And God said, "This is good."

God was happy with his creation. God is the most amazing and creative artist ever. He made such a beautiful world.

On day four, God said, "Let there be lights in the sky to give light on earth." The sun appeared to brightly light the daytime. And the moon appeared to give gentle light at night. God also dotted the nighttime sky with lots of twinkling, blinking stars.

Have you ever looked at the night sky and tried to count the stars? One, two, three . . . that's five . . . there's three hundred, one million, two bazillion . . . Nobody can count that high, right? Isn't God awesome? And that was day four.

Guess what God created on day five? Here's a hint: *swim, splash, dive.* God said, "Let the water fill with living creatures." And all the animals that live in the water appeared: whales, dolphins, sea turtles, and crabs. Catfish, clownfish, starfish, and jellyfish.

On day five, guess what else God created? Here's another hint: *flap, swoosh, soar.* God said, "Let there be birds to fly above the earth." And then every bird appeared in the sky: toucans, penguins, peacocks, ducks, geese, bluebirds, and flamingoes.

So, on day five, he created fish and birds. God might have smiled even bigger when he said, "This is good."

Day six may have been the most exciting of all. On the sixth day, God said, "Let the ground produce land animals." God created wild animals, and tame animals, and farm animals. Every animal you've ever seen or read about or heard about—God created each of those on day six.

From armadillos to zebras and everything in between. Beavers. Camels. Dalmatians. Raccoons. Skunks. (Yep, even the smelly ones!) Tigers. Yaks.

God loved all that he created. But guess what he created next on day six? People!

God formed a man and a woman named Adam and Eve. God made them in his *likeness*. That means Adam and Eve were creative and kind and loving like God, and they could talk and think and care about each other.

After God formed Adam and Eve, God's six days of creating were done. When God looked around and saw all that he had made, he said, "This is very good."

Our all-powerful and holy God had created a beautiful, magnificent world.

Reflection

- What's your favorite thing God created?

- If you could create a new animal, what would your animal look like?

- God loves all his creations—the stars, planets, trees, and animals—everything. And he especially loves every person he creates! He loves you and me more than anything.

- Every time we look at a plant or animal or person he created, we can know that God loves them—and you—mightily, with all his heart.

Prayer

Dear God, thank you for the beautiful world you created. You are mighty and holy. Each time I see your sky, water, land, trees, flowers, food, sun, moon, stars, fish, birds, and animals, help me think of you.

Help me remember how much you love me, since you created it all for me to enjoy.

Thank you, God, for loving me more than I can imagine. Amen.

Adam and Eve

Within six days, God created the whole big world.

After God created the animals, he created the first man. God named him Adam. God made a special place for Adam to live, called the Garden of Eden, and he gave Adam the job of taking care of it.

There were lots and lots of trees in the Garden of Eden with delicious fruit for Adam to eat.

God told Adam, "You can eat the fruit from any of the trees in the garden, except for one. Do not eat the fruit from the tree of the knowledge of good and evil."

God gave Adam another job too, besides taking care of the plants and trees. God let Adam name the animals. (Isn't that job better than washing the dishes?) Camels, donkeys, birds, butterflies, and all the other animals.

Do you ever wonder how Adam could remember all those names? Adam might have said, "Cow. No, wait, I've already used that word. I'll call this one a platypus."

Even though Adam had many animals to hang out with in the Garden of Eden, God knew Adam needed another human in the world.

God created the first woman, and her name was Eve. Together, Adam and Eve took good care of their beautiful Garden of Eden. They had everything they needed, right there in the garden. God had provided everything they could ever need or want.

What happened next is a sad part of Adam and Eve's story.

One day, while Adam and Eve worked in the garden, a sneaky, evil *serpent* tricked Eve. (A serpent is another name for a snake.) The serpent said, "Did God really say, 'You must not eat from any of the trees in the garden'?"

Eve told the serpent that they could eat from any tree, except from the tree of the knowledge of good and evil. She said, "God told us, 'You must not touch it, or you will die.'"

Eve knew God's rule. And Adam knew God's rule. God wanted them to obey him, but when he created man and woman, he gave them the ability to make their own decisions, to choose right from wrong. Sadly, their human nature let them choose wrong this time. They listened to the tricky serpent instead of God.

The snake said, "You won't die. You'll be more like God."

The serpent lied to Eve. He tricked her into tasting fruit from the tree of the knowledge of good and evil—the one tree God had told them not to eat from.

Eve gave fruit to Adam, and he ate some with her. Adam broke God's rule too.

Adam and Eve sinned. They knew it was wrong to eat the fruit, from the very first bite! (Don't you think it was hard to swallow that bite of fruit?) Adam and Eve were so upset about their sin that they hid from God. They were afraid.

When you sin and make bad choices, do you get scared? Does your heart race? Is it hard for you to swallow? Does your voice squeak and crack when you try to talk? I'll bet all those things happened to Adam and Eve.

When God came looking for Adam, God asked him if he'd eaten from the forbidden tree.

"Eve gave me some fruit, and I ate it." Adam blamed Eve for his sin.

When God asked Eve if she had sinned, she blamed the serpent. "The serpent tricked me," she said.

Adam and Eve hurt God when they sinned. God is holy and perfect and good, and he despises sin. God wants us to obey him and be good. God knows what is best for us, and he wants us to choose right instead of wrong.

Because Adam and Eve sinned, God told them they could no longer live in the Garden of Eden.

Our sins hurt God. Our sins hurt us. And most of the time, our sins hurt other people too. God has rules because he knows what is best for us. God loves us so much that he wants us to obey him.

Even though Adam and Eve had to leave the Garden of Eden, God still loved them very much. Our sins hurt God and make him sad. But God will always love us, no matter what.

Reflection

- Why is it sometimes hard for people to do the right thing?

- Why is it sometimes easy to blame someone else when we do wrong, like Adam and Eve did?

- When we choose to sin—like lying, treating someone unfairly, or disobeying our parents—we hurt God. God is good and perfect and holy. He wants no sin or evil in his presence. God wants us to choose right over wrong, no matter what!

Prayer

Dear God, please forgive me when I do wrong. I know that sin hurts you. I want to do what's right. Please help me choose right instead of wrong.

And when I make a bad choice, help me make it right again.

Thank you that you always love me, God, and that you forgive me when I do wrong. Amen.

Noah's Ark

GENESIS 6:5–9:17

A very long time after Adam and Eve left the Garden of Eden, lots of people lived on the earth.

Sadly, most people on earth made bad choices. They treated each other in mean ways. They took things that didn't belong to them. Many of them hurt others with their unkind words. They even killed one another.

Evil and sin filled the earth. All that sin made God sad.

But there was one man who loved God. The man's name was Noah.

Noah made good choices instead of bad ones. Noah obeyed God. God was pleased with Noah because he was a kind and loving man.

God decided to start all over again with the people on the earth. He planned to destroy all of them because of their wicked ways. But he would save Noah. God said to Noah, "I'm going to put an end to all the evil people. I'm going to put an end to their sin. But I will save you and your whole family."

God decided he would bring a terrible flood to the earth. So, he told Noah to build a huge boat. God called it an *ark*. The ark needed to be big enough for Noah, Noah's wife, their three sons—named Shem, Ham, and Japheth—and their wives. Plus, some special passengers would be in the ark with them. God said, "Make the boat large enough to hold two of every kind of animal—one male and one female."

Noah worked for years and years to build the ark. It was a really big task, and Noah obeyed everything God said. He built the boat with a lower deck, a middle deck, and a top deck.

He made a roof for the boat.

He put a door in the side.

And Noah gathered food for every animal. He did just what God told him to do.

Don't you suppose people thought Noah was a little crazy for building a giant boat in his backyard? Do you think he got a sinking feeling every time he saw a neighbor coming his way? (Get it? *Sinking* feeling?) Surely his neighbors laughed at him every time he added a new wooden board to the boat! Their jokes probably hurt Noah.

But Noah's faith never swayed. He stayed strong and trusted his God.

When Noah had finished the ark, God sent two of every animal, one male and one female, to Noah. What a sight to see—a long line of animals marching into the boat!

After the animals were all in the ark, Noah, Noah's wife, Shem, Ham, and Japheth, and their wives got on board.

And then God shut the door.

Drip.

Drip.

Drip.

Rain began to fall from the sky.

It rained. And it rained. And it rained.

No one on earth had ever seen this much rain before.

Inside the ark, birds and animals chirped and squawked and barked and howled. They ate and ate and made big messes. It must have been a smelly, noisy, crowded, stinky boat! It's a wonder anyone could sleep on that floating zoo!

For 40 days, rain fell, until water covered the entire planet. All the people and animals outside the ark perished. Inside the ark, Noah, his family, and all the animals stayed safe and dry.

After the rain stopped, it took a long time for the water to go away. Noah and his family waited and waited inside the ark.

Finally, after many months, Noah sent out a raven. But the bird flew back and forth because it found no trees or dry ground to land on. Then Noah sent out a dove. Like the raven, the dove didn't find anyplace to land. There was still too much water. The dove returned to Noah in the ark.

In another week, Noah sent out the dove again. This time it came back with an olive leaf!

In one more week, Noah sent out the dove again. When it didn't return, Noah knew it was safe for everyone to leave the ark.

Noah worshipped God and thanked him for saving his family.

God told Noah he would never again flood the earth. He made a *covenant* with Noah—that means a promise that God will never break. He said, "I will never flood the whole earth again and destroy all life."

God put a rainbow in the sky as a sign of his promise.

Reflection

- What's the strangest thing your parents or teacher ever told you to do?

- Did you obey? And did you understand the strange request much later?

- Noah didn't really understand what God wanted him to do, but Noah obeyed God.

- People around us might not listen to God. They might make bad choices. But, with God's help, we can choose to do right. And we can encourage others to do what is right too.

Prayer

Dear God, bless me with the strength and faith of Noah. Help me be strong if others try to poke fun at my faith in you.

Lead me to trust your words and obey you. Even when others around me are making bad choices, help me to honor you and do what is right.

I love you, God. Amen.

The Tower of Babel

When Noah and his family left the ark, God told them to spread out all over the earth. God wanted his children to fill the entire world. Noah's sons had children, and those children grew up and had kids. And those kids grew up and had kids. More and more people lived on the earth.

But, just like before, some of the people disobeyed God.

"Let's settle here in Shinar," some of them said. "Let's make our own city. And let's build a really tall tower that reaches to the heavens."

Say what? What were they even thinking? They didn't have elevators back then. How could they climb that many stairs anyway?

You see, the people were filled with *pride*. Pride means thinking too much of yourself and not thinking about God or other people.

The people who planned to build the tower wanted others to think they were special and important. They thought if they built a tower high into the sky, others would say, "Wow, look how great they are." And then, the people of Shinar figured, they would never have to move anywhere else and fill the earth, like God had told them to do.

The people made bricks for the tower. One brick. Stacks of bricks. Piles of bricks. Brick after brick after brick. All the people spoke the same language back then, so it was very easy to talk to each other about the plans for the tower.

"Pack dirt and mud together to make more bricks," someone might have said in the common language.

"Bake them in a hot oven for two hours," another person might have said.

"Take these bricks and start building," another person might have said in that same language.

The people worked so hard to build the tower that their pride and selfishness got in the way of serving God.

God came to see the city and tower that the people were building. He felt disappointed in the prideful people. Just like before, the sin of the people made God sad.

God is good. He is perfect and holy. God wants his children to make right choices. He knows what is best for his people, and he wants them to obey him.

Almost immediately, God decided to put a stop to the tower. And he had an idea. He knew that if he caused the people to speak in different languages, they wouldn't be able to communicate with each other. If they couldn't talk to one another in

the same language about the tower, they couldn't finish building the tower to the heavens.

So, that's just what God did.

He gave this person one language and that person another language.

Suddenly, everyone was speaking in different languages. They couldn't understand each other.

Everyone was confused about what to do next. They stopped building the city and the tall tower.

The people who did talk the same went to one place together. Another group of people who spoke the same language went to another place together. And another group went to a different place to live. The people spread out and scattered all over the earth. Just like God had wanted the people to do in the first place! Just like he had told them to do.

Wouldn't it have been better if the people had simply listened to God? Then they could've skipped all that brickmaking.

That place became known as *Babel*, a word that meant "confused." All the people became confused when God gave them different languages. They couldn't understand each other.

And that tall tower that the people had wanted to reach the heavens? Well, it didn't get very tall at all! God made sure of that.

Reflection

- Do you remember a time when you wanted your way really badly?

- Did your selfishness make you behave unkindly?

- If we're not careful, selfishness can pile up, like a ton of heavy bricks!

- God loves us so much that he wants us to listen to him and obey him. He has a plan for us, and that plan is good. He knows what is best.

- What helps you listen to God and obey?

Prayer

Dear God, help me always listen to you. Help me pray often and never get so busy doing my own thing that I forget about you.

Help me not to be selfish or prideful, because that hurts you and other people, and it hurts me too.

Thank you, God, for Bible stories that teach me to obey you and to make good choices. Amen.

God Calls Abram

GENESIS 12:1–9; 15:5–6;
17:5, 15; 18:1–15; 21:1–7; 22:1–18

After people moved away from the Tower of Babel, more and more men, women, and children lived on the earth. God loved everybody back then, just like he does now. God wanted them to love and obey him too.

God wanted to show the people the right way to live. He picked out one man to do that. That man's name was Abram.

One day, God said to Abram, "I want to make you into a great nation. I want you to be the father of many descendants. I will bless the whole world through you."

Abram might have thought, *What is God talking about? How can I become the father of a great nation? I don't even have children!* You see, Abram and his wife, Sarai, were old by now and childless. They thought they could never have any kids.

God also told Abram to leave his home and go to a land far, far away.

Leave their home? Abram and Sarai had lived with Abram's father in one place for a long time.

That must have been very hard for Abram to leave his family and travel to a new location with just his wife (and one nephew).

And it must have been hard for him to believe he could become the father of a nation when he didn't have any kids.

But Abram did just that! He packed up all his belongings and obeyed God.

Do you know why he did that? Because Abram trusted God. He believed God's promises. He knew God would do what he said. If God said Abram was going to become the father of a nation, then Abram knew he would become the father of a nation. Abram trusted God, just like that.

Sometimes, life was difficult for Abram and Sarai. There were famines and hard times and more moves, but Abram kept trusting God. Abram even had to rescue his nephew, Lot, from bad people.

Abram and Sarai still had no children. But he just kept trusting in God's promises.

God showed Abram the stars in the sky and said, "Your offspring will be as many as the stars in the sky."

Abram had faith in God. He believed that God would do what he'd said.

God changed Abram's name to *Abraham*, which means "father of many." God changed Sarai's name to Sarah.

One day, three visitors came to Abraham. They told Abraham, "By this time next year, you will have a son."

Sarah heard them and laughed. She could hardly believe she would have a son in her old age!

But God reminded Abraham that nothing is too hard for the Lord.

And guess what? One year later, Sarah had a son! They named him Isaac. Abraham and Sarah loved Isaac very much. They were so happy that God had kept his promise and given them a son.

Later, God told Abraham to do something that surprised Abraham. God told him to give up his son Isaac. It was a scary and odd thing God asked Abraham to do. God asked him to sacrifice Isaac. To kill Isaac.

God wanted to be sure that Abraham trusted him completely. Abraham did trust God. He knew that God would take care of his son somehow. Abraham made plans to obey God, but God stopped him.

God said, "Abraham, do not lay a hand on the boy. Now I know you trust me and fear me." (To *fear* God means to make sure you treat God as holy and perfect and good.)

Nearby, Abraham saw a ram caught by his horns in a bush. Abraham sacrificed the ram to God instead of his son.

That was God's way of showing Abraham—and us—that God would one day send his only Son, Jesus, to sacrifice his life to save us.

Abraham trusted God. Sometimes, that was hard to do with the things God asked of Abraham. But Abraham's faith was strong. He trusted God, no matter what.

Reflection

- What's the hardest job your parent or teacher has asked you to do? What's the biggest job you've ever done for God? Sometimes it's difficult to do hard jobs when you don't understand the reason for the job.

- God always knows what's best for us. Even when we don't understand God's plan, we can trust that his plan is good.

- We can be like Abraham. We can trust God too.

Prayer

Dear God, sometimes it's difficult to trust you when things in this world seem hard. Remind me to always trust you, no matter what.

Help me to know without a doubt that you will keep your promises to me, like you did for Abraham.

Thank you, God, that you will always love me and take care of me. Amen.

Rebekah

Abraham lived many more years, and God blessed him. By now, Isaac was grown up, and Abraham knew it was time to pick a wife for Isaac.

Back in those days, families often helped choose who their adult children would marry.

Remember that Abraham now lived in the place where God had sent him. Abraham didn't want to pick a wife from this new country. Instead, Abraham wanted a wife for his son who believed in God and loved God.

So, Abraham told his servant to go back to Abraham and Sarah's long-ago home in the old country to find a wife for Isaac.

Abraham remembered God's promise that God would give Abraham and his offspring this land. Isaac had to stay there too because this was where God wanted his chosen people to live.

The servant traveled a long way, back to Abraham's old home. He took 10 camels loaded with gifts for the new wife's family—gold and silver jewelry and other good things.

The servant had no idea how he was going to pick a wife for Isaac. He wanted to please his master, Abraham. He also trusted God, just like Abraham did. So the servant prayed to God, asking God to show him just the right wife for Isaac.

When he came near Abraham's old homeland, he saw a spring of water, like a pond, with lots of women nearby. In those days, women carried jars to a well or river to get water for their families and their animals. It was hard work for the women to carry those heavy jars of water. They had to make a lot of trips to get enough for everyone.

The servant trusted God to show him the right wife for Isaac. He had an idea. The servant prayed, "God, I'm going to ask a woman for a drink of water. If she is the right wife for Isaac, let her say, 'Drink, and I'll get water for your camels too.'"

Wasn't that a strange prayer? The servant wanted a good wife for Isaac. Perhaps the servant knew that a young woman willing to give water to all his camels had to be a very kind woman, indeed.

And that's just how it happened! The servant asked a young woman for a drink of water.

She said, "Drink," and gave the servant a drink from her jar. Then she said, "I'll fill the water jar for your camels too."

She went back and forth, gathering enough water for 10 thirsty camels.

The servant gave the woman a beautiful gold nose ring and two gold bracelets. He asked about her family and asked if he could spend the night at her family's house.

The girl said, "I am Rebekah, and my father has room for you to spend the night."

The servant discovered that Rebekah's family was part of Abraham's family. He knew that this would delight his master, Abraham. He praised God for showing him the right wife for Isaac.

Rebekah's brother, Laban, came to the spring. The servant told Laban about Abraham and Isaac.

"I came to get a wife for my master's son," the servant said. "My master made me promise to get a wife from his family's clan." The servant told Laban that God had led him to Rebekah. The servant told him about the water for the camels.

Laban knew that it was God's plan for Rebekah to be Isaac's wife. Laban didn't want to say no to God.

The servant gave Rebekah and her family the gifts that he had brought on the camels.

Laban and Rebekah's mother asked Rebekah what she thought about leaving to go marry Isaac.

Rebekah trusted God. She might have been scared to leave her home and go live in a strange land, but she knew this was God's plan for her. Rebekah showed great courage and trust when she said, "I will go with this man to be Isaac's wife."

After the long journey, Rebekah became Isaac's wife. She loved Isaac, and Isaac loved Rebekah.

God had made sure Abraham's offspring would live in the new land. He'd made a very good plan.

Reflection

- What's the bravest thing you've ever done?

- What helped you have courage to do that brave task?

- Rebekah trusted God to do something hard—leave her own family behind and go to a new land and new family. God's plans are always best, even when it means doing something hard. Rebekah knew that God would be with her wherever she went.

- God can help us have the courage to do hard things, just like Rebekah.

Prayer

Dear God, please give me the courage to be brave like Rebekah. Help me do hard things that you want me to do, even if I'm scared.

Thank you, God, that you are always with me no matter where I go. Amen.

Jacob and Esau

GENESIS 25:19–34; 27:1–45; 28:5; 33:4

For a long time, Isaac and Rebekah didn't have any children.
Isaac prayed and asked God for children. God answered Isaac's
prayer.

While Rebekah was pregnant, she felt the baby tossing
and turning inside her. She said to God, "What in the world is
happening?"

God told Rebekah, "Two nations are in your womb. One
group of people will be stronger than the other. The older will
serve the younger."

Well, like always, if God says it, it will happen.

Rebekah didn't have just one baby in her womb. She had
two babies. That's what caused all that jostling inside her!

The first baby had reddish skin and hair all over his body.
They named him Esau. Jacob was born second.

The brothers were very different and didn't really get along.
Esau liked to hunt and work outside. Their father, Isaac, liked
him the best. Jacob liked to work at home, helping his mom
do things around the tents to take care of the family. Rebekah
loved Jacob the best.

God doesn't want moms and dads to have favorites. God wants parents to love all their children the same. God loves all his children the same. He loves us with an *unconditional* love. That means he loves us no matter what. He loves us because he created us. He promises to love us forever and ever.

But our sin makes God sad, even though he always loves us. And just like a good father, God disciplines us for our sins. God will always forgive us, if we ask, but things still happen to us because of our sin. Those things are called *consequences*. When we sin, we have to deal with the consequences of our sins.

Jacob and Esau made some bad choices. One day, when Esau came home from hunting all day, he was tired and hungry. He could smell Jacob's stew cooking, even before he got back to the tent.

"I am starving," Esau told Jacob. "Please give me some of that stew."

Jacob told Esau that he could have some stew . . . *if* Esau gave Jacob his *birthright*.

That's a big word that was really important in Bible days. The firstborn son received a birthright, which means he got more of the father's land and money, plus a position of leadership in the family. In return, he had more jobs and tasks as the firstborn.

And guess what Esau did? He sold his birthright to Jacob for one bowl of stew.

Would you give up your home and land just for a bowl of stew? Even a bowl of your favorite stew?

Jacob made a bad choice too. He was sneaky. When his brother, Esau, had been hungry and tired, he'd tricked Esau into giving him their family's home and land. And those didn't rightfully belong to Jacob.

Later, when their elderly father was dying, Jacob pretended to be Esau so that he could get Esau's special *blessing* from their father too.

In those days, fathers who were about to die gave their children special blessings. Isaac had a blessing for Esau. He had a different blessing for Jacob.

Here is what happened. Because Isaac was dying, he wanted to bless Esau. Their mom heard this. After Esau left to go hunting, their mom told Jacob to wear some of Esau's clothes. And she put goat skins on Jacob's arms so they would feel hairy like Esau's arms.

Isaac had gone blind in his old age, so he could no longer see anyone. Jacob went to his father and lied. He said, "I am Esau. Please give me my blessing."

This was another bad choice for Jacob.

And so, Isaac unknowingly gave Esau's blessing to Jacob.

When Esau came home from the fields and found out what Jacob had done, he was angry. Esau was so angry that he wanted to kill Jacob.

Rebekah wanted to protect Jacob. She told him to move away.

Jacob and Esau had both made bad choices. Rebekah had made bad choices too. They all had to live with the consequences of their sins.

Over time, God helped the brothers change so that they could forgive each other. And much later, when the brothers saw each other again, they did forgive each other and hugged. They finally treated each other with kindness, like family members should.

Reflection

- Can you think of a time when you made a bad choice, and that bad choice caused a serious consequence? Like, maybe sneaking an extra cookie for dessert and then you had a stomachache later?

- Our sins sometimes cause awful consequences.

- When we make bad choices, we can ask God for forgiveness. When we ask for forgiveness, God always forgives.

- We can ask others to forgive us too. God wants all of us to forgive each other, just like he forgives us.

Prayer

Dear God, please keep me from making bad choices. I know my bad choices make you sad. I know my bad choices can hurt me too. Thank you, God, for forgiving me when I do bad things.

Help me forgive others when they hurt me. And help me try extra hard not to hurt other people with my words or actions.

Help me chose right from wrong. Amen.

Rachel and Leah

GENESIS 29–30:34; 32:28; 35:16–26

Jacob left his home because he feared Esau. Jacob had taken Esau's birthright and his blessing, and Esau wanted to kill Jacob. Jacob went to his Uncle Laban's house. Laban let him stay there and work with him.

Laban had two daughters. The oldest was Leah. The Bible says she had "weak eyes." The Bible says that Laban's younger daughter was very beautiful. Her name was Rachel. Some people assume this means Rachel was prettier than Leah.

That must have been hard for Leah to know that everyone thought her younger sister was prettier. Just like Jacob and Esau had brother problems, Rachel and Leah had sister problems.

Jacob worked hard for Laban while he lived with him. After a month, Laban said, "You can't keep working for free. I need to pay you. What wages do you want?"

Jacob was in love with Rachel. Jacob asked Laban if he could have Rachel for his wife.

Laban said, "Work for me for seven years, and then you can have Rachel for your wife."

Jacob loved Rachel so much that he was happy to work for seven years. But at the end of the seven years, Laban tricked Jacob.

It seems there were a lot of sneaky tricks going on in their whole family. Jacob tricked Esau to get his birthright. And Jacob tricked their father, Isaac, to get Esau's blessing. Rebekah helped her son Jacob trick his father, Isaac.

And now, Rebekah's brother, Laban, was tricking Jacob.

Sadly, those same sneaky, tricky sins still happen in the world today.

On the night Jacob was supposed to marry Rachel, Laban brought to him Leah instead of Rachel, and it was so dark, Jacob couldn't see who he was marrying. The next day, he found out he had married Leah instead.

Jacob spoke to his new father-in-law and said, "You promised that I could marry Rachel!"

Laban said, "It is our custom for the oldest daughter to marry first. Work seven more years, and you can marry Rachel too."

In those days, men sometimes had more than one wife. Jacob wanted to marry Rachel. He agreed to work seven more years.

Leah knew that Jacob loved Rachel best. Leah felt unloved. Her own father had tricked Jacob into marrying her.

God saw that Leah felt unloved. Remember, God loves all his children the same. He doesn't have favorites. Because God

knew that Leah felt unloved, he gave her the special blessing of having several children.

At first, Leah wanted to have more and more kids because she thought that would make Jacob finally love her. Leah was jealous of Rachel because Jacob did love Rachel. And Rachel was jealous of Leah because Leah had children, but Rachel had no children yet.

The sisters were jealous of each other. They treated each other harshly. They fought and bickered.

Finally, Leah realized what was most important—God. Even though Leah felt sad that Jacob loved Rachel best, Leah knew it was more important that God loved her. God loved her even though she wasn't as pretty as Rachel. God loved her even though her father had tricked Jacob into marrying her. God loved Leah, and Leah loved God.

She named her fourth son "Judah" and said, "I will praise the Lord." Leah had learned what was most important of all! Years later, it would be through this son, Judah, that God's Son, Jesus, would be born.

Leah and Rachel still fought and bickered. God gave Leah more children. God also gave Rachel two sons before she died. And before Rachel died, God changed Jacob's name to Israel.

Jacob's 12 sons were part of God's plan. Their families would become the 12 *tribes* of Israel, the chosen people that God had promised he would give Abraham through his offspring.

Even though Leah and Rachel sinned by treating each other unkindly, God loved them both the same. The two sisters were also an important part of God's plan for his chosen people.

Reflection

- How would you describe your outer appearance— what you look like when you look in a mirror?

- What words would you use to describe what you feel inside?

- The story of Leah and Rachel teaches us that God looked at their hearts and what they felt inside. God helped Leah see that he was most important of all to her. She finally realized she was special to God.

- You and I are special to God too. We're all part of God's big plan.

Prayer

Dear God, Leah and Rachel's jealousy caused so many problems. Keep me from being jealous of other people.

Remind me not to judge myself or others by their outside appearance, whether they are good looking or not as good looking. Lead me to look at their heart, like you do.

Thank you that you love me, and help me love you always, because that's most important of all. Amen.

Joseph and His Brothers

GENESIS 35:23–26; 37; 39–41:40

Jacob had 12 sons. That's a house full of boys, right? Reuben was the oldest son. Then came Simeon. After him, more sons were born named Levi, Judah, Dan, Naphtali, Gad, Asher, Issachar, and Zebulun. Joseph was the first son Jacob had with his wife Rachel. Joseph was son number 11. Benjamin came last, and he was Rachel's son too.

Because Jacob loved Rachel more than Leah, Jacob also loved Rachel's son Joseph more than he loved Leah's sons.

Joseph's older brothers were jealous of Joseph.

Jacob made his son Joseph a fancy robe with lots of colors. That made the brothers even more jealous.

Joseph made the mistake of telling his older brothers about two dreams that he had. The dreams seemed to say that Joseph would rule over his brothers and that all of them would bow down to him.

That was a bit boastful, right? Joseph might have been better off if he'd kept those dreams to himself.

One day, Jacob sent Joseph to check on his older brothers, who were in the fields grazing their father's flocks. Can you

believe that Joseph wore that fancy robe to check on his brothers? They could see a person coming from far away and recognized Joseph by the robe. That made the brothers very angry. So angry that they decided to kill him.

Reuben didn't want to kill his brother. He talked the others into throwing Joseph into a pit instead. Reuben planned to come back later and rescue him.

The men took Joseph's coat off him and then threw him into the pit.

Some traders came by on their way to Egypt. "Let's sell him to the traders," one of the brothers said, and they did.

After the traders took Joseph away, his older brothers ripped his special coat and put animal blood on it to make it look like Joseph was dead. They took the coat home to show their father and lied to him about Joseph. Jacob's heart felt broken after that.

Meanwhile, in Egypt, Joseph worked as a slave for a rich man named Potiphar. Potiphar was the captain of the guard for the king of Egypt.

You might think that Joseph felt sad and lonely, but he trusted God to take care of him. He worked hard and found favor with Potiphar. God blessed Joseph for trusting him and for working hard. Joseph got a promotion and became Potiphar's assistant.

Just when things were looking up for Joseph, another bad thing happened. Potiphar's wife told a lie about Joseph. That got Joseph in big trouble! Potiphar threw him into prison.

I'll bet you're thinking, *This kid has some really bad luck.*

Joseph just kept right on trusting God and working hard. He worked so hard in prison that the prison warden put him in charge of the whole jail. Joseph prospered, even in prison.

Joseph the dreamer met the pharaoh's cupbearer and baker in prison. They'd made the king angry, and he'd sent them to jail. Joseph listened to the cupbearer's strange dream, and he listened to the baker's strange dream. He told them what their dreams meant. Both dreams happened just like Joseph had said they would.

A couple of years later, Pharaoh, the king of Egypt, had a dream that no one could interpret. The cupbearer remembered Joseph and told the king about him.

The king sent for Joseph and told him his dream about seven healthy cows and seven skinny cows. He also told Joseph his other dream about healthy grain and scorched, or dried-up, grain.

Joseph called upon God to help him know what the dreams meant. He told Pharaoh, "God will help me interpret the dreams." Joseph listened to what God revealed to him about the dreams. Then Joseph said, "God has shown Pharaoh what he is about to do. Rain will fall, and the harvest will be plenty for seven good years. Then a terrible seven-year famine will come to the land."

Joseph told Pharaoh to harvest and save up grain during the seven-year time of plenty. Then Egypt would have enough food for the seven years of famine.

"Great idea," Pharaoh said. "Since God told you all these things, I will put you in charge. There is no one wiser than you to do the job."

Now that really is a promotion. From prison to the palace!

Reflection

- Can you remember a recent time when you felt lonely or sad?

- What helped you know that God was still with you?

- Bad things kept happening to Joseph, but he never stopped trusting God. Joseph never stopped praying or talking to God. He worked hard and made good choices. And he knew that God was always with him.

- God always cares for us. He promises to be with us every minute of every day.

Prayer

Dear God, lead me to trust you, even when hard things or bad things happen to me. Help me know that you are always with me.

Thank you that you promise never to leave me. Amen.

Joseph Sees His Brothers Again

GENESIS 41:41-57; 42-45; 50:15-21

After Joseph told Pharaoh the meaning of his dreams, Pharaoh put Joseph in charge of the whole land of Egypt.

Joseph collected all the extra food during the years of plenty. He stored lots of grain in the cities. Joseph and his wife had two sons, Manasseh and Ephraim. Joseph said he chose those names because God helped him forget all his troubles and because God made Joseph fruitful in the land of his suffering.

Joseph always thought of God. He praised God for the good things God did for him while he was in Egypt. And he trusted God during the hard times.

Soon the famine arrived, and food stopped growing. Joseph began to sell the grain he had collected. People came from all over the world to buy grain from Joseph.

Even Joseph's brothers came to Egypt to buy food. Joseph recognized his brothers, but they didn't know who he was. He was dressed like an Egyptian, and he spoke the Egyptian language. The brothers bowed to Joseph. This made Joseph remember his dreams from years ago. His dreams really had come true!

Joseph was eager to learn more about his brothers, especially his younger brother, Benjamin. They said their youngest brother hadn't traveled to Egypt. He'd stayed home with their father.

Joseph tricked the men at first. Speaking to them through an interpreter, Joseph called his brothers spies. He told the men that one of them would have to stay behind in prison, while the other brothers went back home to get their youngest brother to prove they weren't spies.

The brothers thought God was punishing them because of what they had done to their brother Joseph years before.

The men bought grain and returned home to their father. Except for Simeon. Joseph made him stay behind in jail.

The men told their father that the leader of Egypt wanted Benjamin to go there. Jacob, whose name was now Israel, felt scared that he might lose Benjamin just like he had lost Joseph. He didn't let the brothers go back at first. But when they had eaten all the grain, he sent the brothers again. This time, he sent Benjamin too.

Joseph was so happy to see his younger brother! He called for a big banquet for all of Israel's sons. After the feast, he sent the brothers away with grain. But Joseph tricked the men again. He told one of his servants to hide Joseph's silver cup in Benjamin's grain sack.

Joseph wanted to see if his brothers had changed. He wanted to know if they were still jealous men or if they actually cared about their brother Benjamin.

When Benjamin found the silver cup, the brothers were afraid. But they did the right thing and went back to tell the leader of Egypt what had happened.

The brothers begged Joseph not to punish Benjamin. Judah even said he would remain in Egypt in Benjamin's place and be Joseph's slave. He asked Joseph to let Benjamin return safely to their father.

Then Joseph knew the brothers really loved Benjamin. He knew the brothers loved their father, Israel, too. Joseph finally said, "I am Joseph, your brother. The one you sold as a slave."

The brothers couldn't believe that Joseph was still alive! They also couldn't believe that Joseph wasn't angry with them.

How do you think you would've felt at that moment? Would you rather stay angry and bitter, or forgive and hug and cry a little and then move on?

Joseph said, "Do not be upset. God sent me to Egypt to save lives during the famine. God sent me here to save your lives too. God had a plan all along. Now, go and bring my father here to live. There is plenty of food here!"

Joseph's whole family moved to Egypt. And, wow, was that a happy reunion! Joseph and his father hugged and cried and hugged and cried.

Joseph took care of his brothers, their families, and his father. He gave them the best land to live on. He gave them food to eat during the famine.

Later, when Israel became sick and died, the brothers feared that Joseph would punish them for selling him as a slave long ago. They begged Joseph to forgive them for being so mean.

Joseph cried tears of joy because of his brothers' kindness. He told them, "Do not be afraid. You meant to harm me, but God meant all these things for good. God wanted me to save people's lives. God had a plan."

Reflection

- Think back to a time when something bad happened to you. How did God turn that bad time into something good?

- Sometimes bad things happen to us. Someone in our family might get sick, or a parent might lose a job, or a friend may be really mean to us. God can turn those bad things into good.

- God uses those hard times to bring glory to his name and to bless us.

Prayer

Dear God, help me remember that you can turn around the bad things that happen to me and make them into good things. You can bring good out of anything. When bad things happen, you have a plan.

Remind me that you can use bad things to bring glory to your name and to bless me and others.

And, just like Joseph, help me to forgive anyone who hurts me. Amen.

Miriam Helps Baby Moses

EXODUS 1:1–2:10; 6:20

Israel, who used to be called Jacob, and all his family lived in Egypt with Joseph. The sons of Israel and their families were happy to be in Egypt together, even after Israel died.

Years went by. Another pharaoh became king. The new king wasn't as kind to Joseph's family as the other king. The new king grew to despise the children of Israel. He thought there were too many of them. He was afraid they might try to take over the kingdom of Egypt.

Then Pharaoh decided to mistreat the *Israelites*. (Israelites was another name for the children of Israel.) Pharaoh turned all the Israelites into slaves. He made them work hard for the Egyptian people. The Israelites worked hard in the fields to produce food. They worked hard to make bricks, and then they built buildings using the bricks they had made.

It was hot, tiring, hard work.

The people of Egypt were harsh masters. The king hoped if he worked the Israelites too hard, they would become weak and die.

But God was with the Israelites. All the hard work made them stronger. They had more and more children.

Then Pharaoh had another idea, one that was even more terrible. "Let's kill all the Israelite baby boys," he said.

One Israelite woman, named Jochebed, gave birth to a baby boy. She hid the baby for three months. When she could hide him no longer, she made a basket for the baby, a basket that would float on water. She put the baby into the basket and placed the basket at the edge of the river, among the tall grasses.

The baby's big sister, Miriam, hid nearby and watched.

What words do you think Miriam prayed as she watched her baby brother, tucked into a basket, bouncing in the river's ripples?

Swish. The basket swayed back and forth on top of the water. And Miriam peeked at the basket from her hiding spot.

Swish. Splash.

Miriam saw Pharaoh's daughter coming to the river to bathe.

Do you think Miriam's heart started racing? Do you think she was frightened? How would you have felt at that very moment? Do you think she wanted to run away and not get caught near the basket?

Pharaoh's daughter heard the baby crying and spotted the basket. Pharaoh's daughter looked into the basket at the tiny boy. She felt sad for the crying baby.

Miriam thought of a way to help her baby brother. Boldly, Miriam stepped out from behind the bushes and walked right up to Pharaoh's daughter. Miriam asked, "Would you like me to find a nurse? One who can take care of the baby for you?"

Pharaoh's daughter agreed. She told Miriam, "Yes, go."

Miriam ran as fast as her legs could carry her, all the way home, to get her mother.

"Come quick," she said. "Pharaoh's daughter wants to talk to you!"

Jochebed went quickly with Miriam back to the river. "I'm here. I'm here," Jochebed said. She must have been out of breath from hurrying.

Pharaoh's daughter asked Jochebed to take care of the baby until he was old enough to live with her at the palace.

Miriam helped her mother care for her baby brother. When the boy grew older, their mother took him to Pharaoh's daughter.

Pharaoh's daughter raised him as her own son. She named him *Moses*, which means "to draw out," because she had drawn him out of the water.

Even though Moses was an Israelite, he grew up in the palace like an Egyptian. His heart hurt to know about the Israelites' harsh treatment. He knew those were his people. It made him sad to watch his people work so hard as slaves.

Years later, Moses would do great things for his people. This was all part of God's big plan to save his chosen people, the Israelites.

And a young, brave girl named Miriam had played a big role in God's amazing plan.

Reflection

- What hard jobs have you done for God?

- What helped you have courage to do that job?

- Miriam was just a young girl. Who would've thought she'd play such a big role? Miriam was one of the heroes of the story of saving baby Moses' life.

- God sometimes uses unlikely people to do big jobs. The story of Miriam helps us know that we can do big jobs for God, just like she did.

Prayer

Dear God, lead me to be brave like Miriam so that I can do big jobs for you. Give me the courage to do big jobs, even if I am a little afraid. Give me a strong faith to trust you when I do those big jobs.

Thank you for taking care of me just like you took care of baby Moses and Miriam.

I love you, God. Amen.

Moses and the Burning Bush

EXODUS 2:11–4:17

Moses grew up in the palace until he was a man. One day, he saw an Egyptian beating an Israelite. That hurt his heart and made him angry. He got so mad that he killed the Egyptian.

When Pharaoh found out what Moses had done, Pharaoh was furious. The king tried to kill Moses, but Moses ran far away to live in the desert. There he learned to work as a shepherd.

That must have been a huge change from living in the palace, right? In the palace, Moses probably had servants who took care of him. Now, Moses took care of stinky sheep. And he slept on the ground in a tent.

Would you rather live in a palace or a tent in the desert?

Moses stayed in the desert a long time. He married a woman named Zipporah, and they had children of their own. By now, the king of Egypt had died, and another mean king had taken his place.

"God, help us!" the Israelites prayed. "Save us from our misery!"

Meanwhile, Moses tended flocks of sheep in the fields. Day after day, the same thing. Feed and water the sheep. Go home and sleep.

But one day, that all changed.

Moses thought he and the sheep were alone in the desert. But suddenly, he saw a bush covered in flames. The bush burned bright and hot, with orange and red fire. The odd thing was the bush never burned up! The leaves were still there—still green and alive—yet the bush kept right on burning.

What in the world is going on? Moses thought.

Moses walked closer to check out the strange happening.

Then things really got weird.

The bush started talking! Well, not really the bush. But a voice came from the bush. "Moses!" the voice said. And again, "Moses."

Moses knew it was the voice of God. Moses answered, "Here I am."

God told Moses, "Do not come any closer. Take off your sandals."

Moses had no idea why he needed to be barefoot.

"The place where you are standing is holy ground," God said to Moses.

Moses took off his sandals. He kept listening to God and watching the bush.

"I am the God of your father, the God of Abraham, the God of Isaac, and the God of Jacob."

Now Moses hid his face. He was afraid to look at God. But he listened to every word God said.

"I have seen the misery of my people in Egypt," God said. "I have heard them cry out from all the harsh, hard work. I know they suffer."

God told Moses that he was going to save his people. He would rescue the children of Israel and bring them to better land.

A long time ago, God had told Abraham to move to that land, and he'd promised Abraham that Abraham's offspring would live there too. God had described it as "a land flowing with milk and honey." That meant plenty of cows could live on the land, and bees, and many people too.

As Moses listened to God talk to him from the burning bush, Moses might have thought, *This is great! God plans to rescue my whole family clan—hundreds of thousands of people—from the country of Egypt!*

But then God said, "And, Moses, I'm sending you to save them."

Moses probably felt like fainting! "Me?" he said. "You want to send me?"

God said, "I will be with you."

Moses was scared. He didn't think he could do this big job that God wanted him to do.

Moses asked God, "What if Pharaoh won't listen?"

God said, "Tell him *I AM* sent you." God said that because "I AM" is the name God gave to describe himself. In the Israelite language, Hebrew, "I AM" sounds like *Yahweh*.

"What if they don't believe me?" Moses asked God.

God told Moses to throw his shepherd's staff onto the ground. Moses did. The stick with its curved end became a snake. Moses shrieked and ran. Then God told him to pick up the snake by the tail. When Moses did, it was a shepherd's staff again.

"See?" God said. "They'll believe that I am God."

Moses didn't think he was up for this job. It seemed impossible. He even used the excuse that he couldn't talk well. "Please send someone else, God."

God told Moses that Moses' brother, Aaron, could go with him. "I will be with both of you," God said. "I will help you know what to say."

Moses was still afraid. But he knew he had to do the job God wanted him to do. It would be a really difficult job, but God had promised to be with him.

Reflection

- Have you ever felt like you weren't the right person to do a certain job? Like, maybe you weren't tall enough or smart enough? How did you get that job done?

- When God wants to use us for a big job, he will help us. He'll give us what we need to complete the task.

- We can trust God to help us. We can trust God to be with us each step of the way.

Prayer

Dear God, thank you for the promise that you will always be with me. Thank you that you help me with all my jobs, with everything that I do. Big jobs, little jobs, and everything in between.

Help me know without a doubt that you are with me. Help me not to be afraid when you ask me to do a job.

Lead me to trust you every day. Amen.

Escape from Egypt

EXODUS 7–14

Moses and his brother, Aaron, went to see Pharaoh, just like God had told them to do.

"Let God's people go," Moses said.

Pharaoh didn't want the Israelites to leave Egypt. Who would do all the hard work if he let them go? The king said, "No. The children of Israel are not leaving."

Moses and Aaron may have thought, *Okay, Pharaoh, you asked for it. Now God will show you his power.*

God decided to send *plagues* to Egypt to prove how mighty he is. Ten plagues in all. (A plague is a bad thing that affects a lot of people, like a really bad illness, or a bug problem, or something even more awful.)

And so, God began.

God told Moses to have Aaron stretch out his wooden staff over the waters. And, POOF! Just like that, all the water in Egypt turned into blood.

Did that convince Pharaoh? Nope. He still wouldn't let the Israelites go.

Moses told Pharaoh, "God said to let his people go, or he'll plague your country with frogs."

Now, frogs don't really seem that bad, right? A *croak,*
croak here. And a *ribbit, ribbit* there. Here a hop; there a jump.
Everywhere a froggy frog.

But God sent millions and millions of frogs. Frogs covered
the land so thickly that no one could see the ground. Pharaoh
and his people suffered because of so many frogs.

Pharaoh said to Moses and Aaron, "If God will take away the
frogs, I'll let his people go."

But Pharaoh lied. After God ended the plague of frogs,
Pharaoh said, "Nope. Now the people can't leave."

Next came a plague of gnats. God told Moses to have Aaron
strike the ground with his staff. POOF! Just like that, every grain
of sand became a gnat. Gnats swarmed all over the people and
animals of Egypt. They could barely breathe because of the
gnats.

When the small bugs didn't get the best of Pharaoh, God
sent bigger insects—flies. The plague of flies pestered the
Egyptians . . . but not the Israelites. That way, God showed that
the children of Israel were his special people.

Pharaoh told Moses and Aaron, "Now God's people can go,
but first pray and ask God to get rid of the bugs." Moses prayed,
and God removed all the bugs. But, once again, Pharaoh took
back his word. He wouldn't let God's people leave.

Next God sent a plague on the livestock of the Egyptian
people. Horses, donkeys, camels, cows, sheep, and goats died.

But not one of the animals that belonged to the Israelites died. Even that terrible plague didn't change Pharaoh's mind.

A plague of sores came next. Painful sores appeared all over the bodies of the Egyptian people and their animals. But Pharaoh said, "No, God's people can't leave."

Next, hail fell from the sky, crushing the crops that had been growing in the fields. Pharaoh still wouldn't let the Israelites leave.

Now God sent even bigger insects. Locusts swarmed the land and ate every plant and tree in sight.

Moses and Aaron told Pharaoh, "Let God's people go so that we may worship him in the desert away from here."

But no. Pharaoh wouldn't give in.

A plague of darkness came next. And after the darkness, the worst plague of all came to the people of Egypt. God said he would kill the firstborn son of every family in Egypt.

But God warned the Israelites to make a sign on their homes. He said that each Israelite family should kill a lamb and prepare a meal. He told them to use some of the lambs' blood and paint it on the doorposts of their houses. He also told them to make flat bread with no yeast as part of their meal.

God said the plague of death would come to the Egyptians. But the sign of blood on the doorposts would make the plague of death *pass over* the homes of the Israelites. None of the Israelites would be hurt.

When death came to the houses of Egypt, weeping and wailing arose all across their country. But all the Israelite families were safe.

Pharaoh finally told Moses and Aaron, "Go, you and all the Israelites. Leave my country. Go and worship your God."

All of God's children left Egypt that day. God used a tall cloud to lead them during the day, and at night, the tall cloud turned into a bright fire to provide light and guide the people. God led the Israelites to camp near the Red Sea.

And guess what happened next? You guessed it! Pharaoh changed his mind. He didn't want his Israelite slaves to be gone from Egypt! So he sent his army to chase down the Israelites and bring them back.

God had *still* more power to show the Egyptians and Israelites! He told Moses to stretch out his shepherd's staff over the Red Sea. Moses did what God said. The sea opened to form a wide path of dry ground to the other shore, with water standing up on the right and on the left like the walls of a hallway.

The children of Israel walked safely across the dry bottom of the Red Sea and escaped Pharaoh's army.

God had moved an entire sea of water for his people.

When all the Israelites were safe on the other shore, God sent the water crashing down to cover the Egyptian army. They didn't chase the Israelites ever again.

God's people were finally free!

Reflection

- What is the most powerful thing you've seen a real person do?

- No one can do the things God can do, not even superheroes. God is much more powerful.

- When God promised his chosen people that he would take care of them, he meant it. God's love for his people never ends.

- God loves you and me with an unfailing love too. God will never stop loving us. Ever.

Prayer

Dear God, I praise you because you are mighty. I praise you because you are powerful. I praise you because there is no other God but you. There is no one who can do the things you can do.

Thank you for saving the Israelites, and thank you for sending Jesus to save me. Thank you that you always love me. Amen.

God Provides in the Desert

EXODUS 15:22-17:7

The children of God were finally free from years and years of slavery. They celebrated with music and songs and dancing. The people praised God. They thanked him for saving them.

All God's people were full of joy.

Until . . .

Shortly after they crossed the Red Sea, the people spent three days traveling in the desert without finding water. Even with all the powerful things God had done for them, the people began to grumble. And pout. And complain.

When they finally found water, it tasted bad. And they grumbled some more.

God showed Moses a piece of wood. When Moses threw it into the water—POOF!—the water tasted good. God was still in the miracle business! He just kept on showing his mighty power to his children.

God said to the people, "Listen to me and do what is right. Keep my commands. Make good choices. Then I will not bring on you the plagues I brought on the Egyptians." God reminded them, "I am the Lord."

God guided them to another place, a wonderful place. There were a dozen springs of water and lots of palm trees for shade. The people camped near the water and stopped grumbling.

Until . . .

When their tummies rumbled from hunger, the people grumbled to Moses. "We need food," they said. "We're going to starve!"

God told the Israelites he would send meat in the evenings and bread in the mornings.

That very evening, quail came and covered the camp. The people were happy again! "Quail for dinner!" they said.

And the next morning, a layer of dew covered the desert floor around them. When the dew drops faded away, they became thin, white flakes that looked like frost. The Israelites had never seen anything like it. When they tasted the flakes, they realized the odd flakes were pieces of yummy bread.

"What is this?" the people asked each other. "What is it?"

No one had ever seen or tasted anything like the bread God sent. So they called it *manna*, which means, "What is it?"

God gave them specific instructions about the manna. He wanted to see if the people would follow his instructions. He also wanted them to know that he would provide for them and take care of them. And white stuff appearing on the ground was how he planned to show them.

God said, "Gather only the amount of manna you can eat in one day. No more." However, on the sixth day, God said they should gather enough for two days. He wanted them to rest from work on the seventh day, just like God had done long ago when he'd created the world.

The people gathered what they would need for the first day. Some gathered extra and tried to keep it overnight, even though God and Moses had told them not to. When those people woke up the next morning, the bread they'd tried to save was full of small bugs called maggots. And the bread smelled bad.

Moses was angry that those people had disobeyed God.

Each morning, God gave everyone new manna. And each evening, the quail came.

On the sixth day, the people gathered enough manna for two days. On the seventh day, the day of rest, God didn't send manna. And guess what? This time, no maggots came to the extra manna. And it tasted delicious! Even though some of the Israelites looked for manna on the seventh day, they found none.

God did just what he said he would do.

And the people stopped grumbling.

Until . . .

When they moved to a new camp, the Israelites couldn't find water.

"Why did you bring us here to die?" the people grumbled.

How could they forget all the times God had taken care of them?

God told Moses to strike a rock with his staff. Moses did. *Smack!* Clean, delicious water flowed right out of the rock.

The people cheered and praised the Lord. The people stopped grumbling.

Until . . .

Reflection

- The last time you grumbled, why were you unhappy?

- God took care of his people. But when something went wrong, they grumbled.

- We can make that mistake sometimes too. God does good things for us, but at the first sign of trouble, we complain.

- God wants us to trust him and not complain. If we need something, simply pray and ask God, without grumbling. God promises to take care of us.

Prayer

Dear God, thank you that you promise to take care of my needs. That doesn't mean that I'll get everything I want. It does mean you are always with me.

Help me not to grumble when things don't go my way. Thank you for all the good things that you do for me. Amen.

The 10 Commandments

EXODUS 19:16–20:17; 31:18

Thunder and lightning. Thick clouds and smoke. A loud trumpet blast. Sounds like a scene from a movie, right?

God was about to do something BIG. He does a lot of big things in the Bible, doesn't he? Who could forget how God created the world in just six days? Who could forget how God led Joseph from slave to prisoner to the second most important man in Egypt?

Who could forget all those plagues—frogs, gnats, locusts, and hail? Surely, everyone remembers how God opened the Red Sea so the Israelites could walk through it on dry ground.

And who could forget how God gave his chosen people manna every morning and quail every night . . . and water from a rock?

But guess what? The people of God forgot those big things.

God knew the people of Israel needed rules to help them remember how important God is. He knew they needed rules to help them live the right way and make good choices. God knew that his people would be happiest if they followed his rules.

So God told Moses to come to him on the top of Mount Sinai because God had something important to tell him.

Moses looked up at the mountain. A thick cloud and smoke covered it. Lightning flashed from the cloud. Thunder boomed from it. Trumpet sounds blasted from the cloud. The whole mountain shook. Moses climbed to the top of the quivering mountain to meet with God.

That must have been a challenge, right? Let's hope he had that staff to hold him steady!

On top of the mountain, God gave Moses important rules. The rules would help the people live the right way and stay safe. The rules would also help the people of Israel show the world that they were God's special people.

God wanted to set apart the nation of Israel to show everyone else in the world how to live.

God was ready to speak to Moses. He gave Moses 10 really important rules first, before he told him many other rules. These 10 rules were so important that God carved the rules with his own finger into large, flat pieces of rock.

We call these rules the 10 Commandments.

Here are the 10 big rules God gave Moses that day on the mountain.

The First Commandment: *Do not worship other gods.*

God is the only God there is. He didn't want his people to worship and honor the fake gods invented by other people in the world.

The Second Commandment: *Do not make idols.*

The Israelites would be moving to the country of Canaan. The people already living in Canaan, and people in other parts of the world, made little statues of the false gods they imagined to be real. They called these statues "idols." God said not to make those or worship them.

Not many people have statue idols today. But we sometimes make a kind of idol out of things, and we shouldn't, because we might love those things more than God. Things like money, fancy clothes, famous movie stars, talented singers, or athletes. We have to be careful not to love any of those things more than we love God. God wants to be first in our lives.

The Third Commandment: *Do not use God's name in bad ways.*

God's name should never be used like a cuss word. When we say God's name, we should speak to him, and about him, with love.

The Fourth Commandment: *Keep the Sabbath day as a holy day.*

Sabbath day means a day of rest. For us, that's usually Sunday. This commandment means that God wants his people to rest from working and also to spend special time with God, worshipping him and talking to him in prayer.

The Fifth Commandment: *Honor your father and mother.*

God expects us to respect our parents. He gave us our parents to love us, care for us, and to help us grow to become kind and loving, like God.

The Sixth Commandment: *Do not murder anyone.*

Killing people is wrong. We should never, ever kill another person.

The Seventh Commandment: *Do not take someone else's husband or wife to be your husband or wife.*

God wants husbands and wives to be true to each other.

The Eighth Commandment: *Do not steal.*

God does not want people to take things that do not belong to them.

The Ninth Commandment: *Do not speak untrue words about other people.*

God wants people to tell the truth. At times, that can be hard to do. But even little lies are wrong. Often, a little lie leads to another lie that leads to still another lie. The lies get bigger and bigger. "Just tell the truth," God said.

The Tenth Commandment: *Do not want something that belongs to someone else.*

God wants us to be content with the things we have. He doesn't want us to be jealous of the things other people have.

God told Moses these 10 Commandments and carved them on flat pieces of stone. God did this so Moses and the Israelites could always keep them and remember them.

He gave Moses many other rules for the people to follow, but these were 10 of the most important rules of all.

Reflection

- Which one of the 10 Commandments is the hardest for you to follow?

- Which one of your parents' or teacher's rules is the hardest for you?

- God gave Moses rules to help people live safely and happily.

- God wanted his chosen ones to show the rest of the world the right way to live. God loves everyone in the world so much that he wants what's best for them. And following God's rules is best!

Prayer

Dear God, sometimes it's hard to follow rules. Because we're humans who make mistakes, we like to do things our own way. But you gave us rules because you know what is best for us. You know that always following your rules will make us the happiest and keep us the safest.

Help me follow rules, God, and be obedient. Help me obey the 10 Commandments because you know what is best for me. Amen.

The 12 Spies

"Pack your sandals and your tents. Grab your children and your cloaks."

God told the people of Israel to pack up their belongings and head toward the Promised Land.

A long time ago, God had told Abraham that he would be the father of a great nation. God had also said that he would one day give the land of Canaan to God's people.

At last, God's people were headed to that wonderful land of milk and honey.

It was a long trek from Mount Sinai, where God had given Moses the 10 Commandments, to the land of Canaan. Once again, God led the people with a tall, white cloud. And guess what? As the people traveled, they grumbled. Again.

"We need meat," somebody said.

"We're tired of eating this white, flaky manna," another one said.

Remember? No one had ever seen that white stuff, so they had given it the name manna because that means "What is it?"

God had also told Moses he would give the people meat. God had sent quail. And so the people ate quail. And more quail the next day. And more quail the next day. Quail, quail, quail, until someone might have begged, "Quit with the quail!"

If you had to eat the same food every day for a really long time, what would you want it to be? Quail? Chicken? Pizza? Wait—pizza hadn't been invented yet!

Finally the people's journey ended. They reached the amazing Promised Land.

God told Moses to send 12 men to explore Canaan. God chose that special number to represent each of the 12 tribes, or families, of Israel.

One from Reuben's tribe.

One from Simeon's tribe.

One from Judah's tribe.

One from Issachar's tribe.

One from Ephraim's tribe.

One from Benjamin's tribe.

One from Zebulun's tribe.

One from Manasseh's tribe.

One from Dan's tribe.

One from Asher's tribe.

One from Naphtali's tribe.

One from Gad's tribe.

The 12 men snuck into Canaan from the south and explored. The men spent 40 days checking out the land and the fruit trees and the people.

"Look at the size of those grapes," one of the men probably said.

"This one is bigger than my head," another guy could have said.

He might have exaggerated just a little.

The men gathered clusters of grapes, handfuls of pomegranates, and bunches of figs to take back with them.

The people of Israel couldn't wait to hear what the spies had to say about the land of Canaan.

"Good golly, what gorgeous grapes," one of the Israelite mamas probably gushed.

"That's a pile of plump pomegranates," one of the Israelite kids might have proclaimed.

"What a find of fresh figs," another child could have fancied.

The people marveled at the amazing fruit.

"The land really does flow with milk and honey," said one of the spies. "Look at this great fruit."

When he spoke again, the people suddenly lost their appetite for juicy fruit.

"But some of the people there are giants!"

Uh oh. That's not the news they wanted to hear!

Ten of the spies gave a bad report. "Too many people live in Canaan," they told the Israelites. "We're not strong enough to take their land." Their words scared God's chosen people.

But two spies, Caleb and Joshua, spoke up. They said, "The land is good! God promised the land to us. We can do this with God on our side. We can live in the land that God promised us. We can trust God."

Two trusted God. Ten didn't trust God.

Would you have chosen Team Caleb and Joshua? Or Team 10 Scared Spies?

Ten men talked the people of Israel out of trusting God. They let fear win instead.

God was angry with the people of Israel. And disappointed. God wanted to teach his chosen people to trust him.

Because many of the people didn't trust God, God said that none of the unbelievers would ever enter the Promised Land. God loved his special people, but he told Moses the people would wander the desert for 40 years as punishment. They could never live in the Promised Land.

Only Caleb and Joshua and the next generation of Israelites would get to live in Canaan one day.

Reflection

- Can you remember a time when you let one of your friends talk you out of being brave?

- What did that person say that made you doubt you could be brave?

- Most of God's people missed out on the Promised Land because they doubted God.

- Even when something seems impossible, we can know that God will always be with us. We don't have to be afraid. We can trust God to do what he promises.

Prayer

Dear God, I know you have big plans for me, just like you had big plans for the people of Israel. Help me not to miss out on those big things because of fear. Lead me to be more like Caleb and Joshua, to trust you and be brave.

Remind me that you are always with me, no matter where I go or what I do. Help me trust your plans and your promises. Amen.

Rahab to the Rescue

NUMBERS 20:2-13; 27:12-23;
DEUTERONOMY 34; JOSHUA 1:1-9; 2:1-21

The Israelites wandered in the desert for 40 years, just like God had said. They camped here for a bit and then packed up and moved there. They camped there for a time and then packed up and moved over yonder.

Camping. Packing. Tromping. Moving. Then repeat.

Quite often, God's chosen people were grouchy. They complained a lot. They forgot about the many ways God took care of them.

Moses never forgot what God did for his chosen people. Moses was a mighty man who led and took care of God's people. Yet even Moses wasn't perfect.

One day, Moses got so tired of hearing the people's complaints that he lost his temper.

Here's what happened.

The people begged for fresh water. God told Moses to speak to a giant rock, and then fresh, clear water would gush out of it. Instead, Moses angrily struck the rock with his staff. Water did pour out of the rock, but Moses had disobeyed God.

Moses was getting old, and he knew that the people would need a new leader. God told Moses to make Joshua the new leader.

After Joshua became the new leader, Moses knew his days were coming to an end. Moses climbed to the top of a mountain, and God let Moses see all the Promised Land. Sadly, Moses couldn't go to the lush land of Canaan because he had disobeyed God.

Moses died there on the mountain. The people cried and grieved.

God spoke to the new leader. "Joshua, get ready to cross the Jordan River."

God also told Joshua, "Be strong and have courage. I will never leave you. I will be with you wherever you go."

Joshua led the people to the river. Across the river stood the strong, sturdy walls of the city of Jericho.

Time for more spies!

Joshua chose two men to cross the river, sneak into the city of Jericho, and spy on the people there. God wanted his people to take the city of Jericho as part of their land.

The two spies got past the walls of the city. "Okay, now what?" they wondered.

Fortunately, a brave woman named Rahab let the two men come inside her house. Many people in Jericho knew that Rahab was a sinful woman. But she wanted to help God's

people. She told the two Israelite men, "I know that the Lord has given you this land. The people of Jericho are afraid. We know what God has done for the people of Israel. We know your God is the only God."

Guards came looking for the two spies. Quick-thinking Rahab told the spies to hide on the roof.

The roof? You might think that's a strange place to hide, but back in those days, most houses had flat roofs. That means no one could stand outside and see whether anyone was on the roof. Now it sounds like a great hiding spot, right?

Where's the best place you've ever hidden?

The two spies climbed to the roof and hid under some large plant leaves. Families often dried flax plants on the roof and then turned the plant fibers into fabric to make clothes.

And you thought you had a tough job, just folding the laundry.

The men's hearts must have pounded like drums as they covered themselves with the dried plants. Rahab's heart must have pounded too when the guards banged on the door, yelling, "Open up! Give us the spies!"

Rahab told the guards that the men left. "Hurry, and you might catch them," she said.

Sneaky, huh?

The guards ran out the door to look for the spies. Rahab climbed to the roof. She told the spies, "You're safe now. The guards went somewhere else to look for you."

"How can we get out of here?" the spies wondered. "The gates are closed."

Well, guess what Rahab just happened to have? A rope!

Rahab helped the men escape through a window of her house. Using the rope, the men safely climbed down outside the Jericho wall. Good thing those two were expert spies AND climbers!

Before the spies left, Rahab begged the men to save her family. The spies said, "Tie a red cord in your window. When we come back, we'll make sure you are safe. Because you helped us, we promise to save your family."

Even though Rahab, a woman with many sins, was not part of God's chosen people, Israel, she believed God and trusted God. She wanted to help God's people.

Reflection

- Have you ever helped someone in trouble?

- How did you help them?

- Sometimes God uses unlikely people to do big jobs. Rahab wasn't an Israelite, but she did big things for God's people when she hid the spies.

- Some people might have wondered how a young woman could get two strong men over those walls, but Rahab knew just how to help them escape. Rahab wasn't perfect, but God chose her to help his people.

Prayer

Dear God, help me be kind to God's people, like Rahab was. Help me trust you, like Rahab did, especially when you have a big job for me to do.

Thank you for Rahab's story, because it teaches me that you can use me for big jobs, despite my faults and sins.

You are the wonderful God of heaven and earth. You are the only God. Thank you for creating me. Amen.

The Walls of Jericho

JOSHUA 2:22-4; 6:1-25

The two spies couldn't wait to get back to the people of Israel and tell them the good news. "The Lord has surely given the land into our hands!" they shouted excitedly. "The people of Jericho are afraid of us. They've heard about our one true God. They know all the good things he did for us in Egypt and in the desert."

This time, the spies trusted God. The people listened to the spies and trusted God too.

Just one problem: Somehow, a lot of men and women and children and cattle and donkeys had to get across the Jordan River.

But God had a plan, like he always does. Nothing takes him by surprise. God didn't say, "What? You mean there's a river blocking the path? Whatever will we do?"

God had a plan. A good one. And . . . it involved another miracle!

If you think this miracle is good, wait until you see the next Jericho miracle. It gets even better. God's miracles are, well, miraculous! God can do mighty and powerful things. But we're getting ahead of our story. Let's get back to the Jordan River miracle.

Joshua gathered all the people of Israel. Now, the priests of Israel were all from the tribe of Levi. Joshua told the priests to lead the way across the Jordan River while carrying the ark of the covenant. The ark of the covenant was God's special wooden box, with two angel statues on top. All of it was covered in gold. The ark contained the stone tablets with the 10 Commandments that God had given to Moses. The priests carried the ark of the covenant with two poles.

Are you ready for the miracle?

As soon as the priests who were carrying the ark stepped into the Jordan River, the water stopped. It stopped flowing upstream from where they stood, and it piled itself into a big, huge wall of water. Now the people could walk across on dry ground.

How cool is that? Do you think the people remembered their parents and grandparents telling them about the other time God did that, when he parted the Red Sea?

The priests, still carrying the ark, stopped in the middle of the riverbed. They stood there and patiently waited until the entire nation of Israel had crossed on dry ground.

Then God told Joshua to have one man from each of the 12 tribes pick up a stone from the middle of the riverbed, right where the priests stood. The men carried the stones to their camp.

Joshua stacked the 12 stones as a memorial to remind the people of God's power. God wanted the people to remember how he had stopped the river from flowing so they could walk on dry ground.

When all the people had crossed the river, the priests with the ark finally finished crossing. As soon as their feet left the riverbed, the water came crashing down in a deafening noise. The river flowed normally again.

On the other side of the river, the Israelites faced another problem. The city of Jericho was surrounded by tall, stone walls and strong gates. No one could get inside the giant city.

But God had a plan. A rather strange plan.

Here's what God told Joshua to do. "For six days, have all the armed men of Israel walk around the walls of the city, one time each day. At the very front of the line, have seven priests lead them while holding trumpets. Behind those priests, have other priests carry the ark of the covenant.

"On the seventh day, march around the city seven times, with the priests blowing the trumpets. Then have the priests sound a long, loud trumpet blast, and have the whole army shout as loud as possible. When they do, the city walls will fall down."

Say what? That sounds like the strangest battle plan ever, doesn't it? What would your idea be to capture the city of Jericho?

God's way might have sounded a little odd, but God always knows best. His plans and ideas are always the right ones.

Not one single person doubted God. The people did exactly what God said.

Day one—one march around the city.

Day two—one march around the city.

Day three—one march around the city.

Day four—one march around the city.

Day five—one march around the city.

Day six—one march around the city.

Day seven—seven laps around the city with the priests blowing trumpets. Then the priests blew the trumpets really loud, and all the Israelite soldiers shouted. "RAAAAH!!!"

Guess what happened? The walls of Jericho came tumbling down, exactly as God had said they would.

The Israelites took control of the city, just like God wanted them to do.

And Joshua remembered the two spies' promise to Rahab. He sent the spies to save her and her whole family.

Reflection

- Has God ever asked you to do something that you didn't understand?

- Was it as strange as marching around a city while yelling?

- Maybe God asked you to sit with the new kid or include someone at recess, even though they are the worst ball player ever.

- The Israelites trusted God, even though his instructions seemed weird. Like the Israelites, we can trust God, even when we don't understand his plan.

Prayer

Dear God, sometimes I don't understand your plans. Sometimes I don't know why you want me to do the things you ask me to do. But, God, I know your plans are always best. Help me to have the courage to march forward with your plans, because I know you will always be with me.

Thank you, God, that you have taught me to trust you. Amen.

Gideon and the Time of the Judges

JOSHUA 8–13; 24:29–31; JUDGES 1–2; 6–7:23

God's chosen people, the Israelites, were finally home. God had promised the land of Canaan to Abraham a long, long time ago. God had told Abraham that his descendants would become a great nation, a chosen nation, for God to show the whole world how to live and love only God.

Even though God gave the land of Canaan to the Israelites, other people groups lived there too. Those people worshipped false gods. They did not worship the one true God.

God didn't want the others living there to have a bad influence on God's people. So, God told the Israelites to drive out everyone from the Promised Land except his special people. That caused wars and fighting.

But, once again, the stubborn Israelites didn't listen to God. They didn't make all the bad people leave Canaan after the wars.

When the Israelites finally had control over the land of Canaan, Joshua divided the land between the 12 tribes of Israel.

God told the Israelites that if they worshipped only him, he would take care of them. He told them not to worship the false gods of the people living around them. Joshua made them promise to worship only God. And they did . . . for a time.

But after Joshua grew old and died, the people of God no longer had a leader. Many of them stopped thinking about all that God had done, and still did, for them.

When the people forgot about God and worshipped false gods, God took his hand of protection away from them. Other nations would come to the land of Israel to fight the Israelites. When the people of God had big trouble, they would remember God and call out to him.

God raised up 12 leaders called *judges*, one at a time, to help the Israelite people in their times of need. But each time, when the trouble was over, the people forgot about God.

One day, trouble showed up, with a capital "M." Midianites. Mean Midianites, to be exact. The Midianites were enemies of God's people. For many years, the Midianites raided the nation of Israel, stealing their food at harvest time and destroying their fields. They came every year to plunder and ravage.

The frightened people of Israel cried out to God again. God sent the angel of the Lord to a man named Gideon. The angel told Gideon that God wanted Gideon to save his people.

Gideon didn't think he could fight the Midianites. "Who, me?" he said. "But my tribe is the weakest tribe. I'm not strong. I can't do it." Gideon didn't feel like a hero. He didn't think he could do the job.

The angel told Gideon that with God's help, Gideon could rescue the Israelites from the invaders. But even before Gideon had time to gather an army of fighters, the angel told Gideon to do something else. "Tear down the altar of the false god. Build an altar to the one true God instead."

God wanted the Israelites to know he was their God. He wanted them to worship only him. And he wanted to be sure they remembered him before going into battle.

Gideon asked for volunteers to fight with him. A lot of soldiers stepped up to fight, but God told Gideon the army was too big.

Gideon must have thought God was joking. "You're kidding, right?" he might have said. "Don't we need a lot of fighters to win the battle?"

But God knew that a huge army might make the Israelites think they'd won the battle on their own, without God's help.

"Nope, too many people," God might have said. "Tell the ones who are frightened to turn away."

When a bunch of men went back home, God said, "The army is still too big."

By now, Gideon was probably shaking in his army boots!

But God had a plan to choose the fighters. He told Gideon to take the men to the water for a drink. Only the men who lapped the water like dogs should stay with Gideon. Those who drank the water by scooping it in their hands should go home. When Gideon counted the men, he had only 300 people in his army.

God said, "With three hundred men, I will give you victory."

And you know what? God did just that. When the battle was over, the Israelites were free from the Midianite bullies.

Reflection

- When is a time that you felt like a hero?

- What did you do that was extra special?

- How did God help you with that task?

- God often uses unlikely heroes to accomplish his plans. That way, God gets the glory.

- Like Gideon, for example. It took huge courage and a lot of trust in God, but Gideon got the job done with God's help.

- God wants you and me to be courageous too.

Prayer

Dear God, big jobs can be scary. Help me trust you to do the big jobs you want me to do. Please give me courage when I am afraid. Lead me to be brave like Gideon.

Thank you for being the one true God. Help me worship only you. Thank you for loving me. Amen.

Ruth and Naomi

RUTH 1–4:13

When a great famine occurred, food was scarce all over the land of Israel. Some families moved to other places to find food.

A man named Elimelek traveled to the country of Moab with his wife, Naomi, and their two sons. They walked a long way to get there, but then they settled in Moab.

After a time, Naomi's husband died. She grieved the loss of her husband. Her sons married women from Moab. One son married a woman named Orpah. The other son married a woman named Ruth.

Naomi lived with her sons and daughters-in-law in the land of Moab for about 10 years. Then Naomi suffered another tragedy. Both of her sons died. That left Naomi, Orpah, and Ruth without husbands. In those days, it was often hard for women to find work. Most women depended on the men in their families to earn money.

When Naomi heard that the famine in Israel was over, she wanted to go back home to the town of Bethlehem, located in a part of the country known as Judah. She had no way to take care of herself in Moab. She hoped life might be better in Judah.

Naomi and Orpah and Ruth packed up their few belongings and started walking toward Naomi's home. Before long, Naomi stopped on the dusty road and turned to her daughters-in-law, whom she loved dearly.

Naomi said, "Please go back to your mothers' homes and live with your own families." She didn't want to lose her daughters-in-law, but she thought it was only fair to let them go back to their own people. She said, "Maybe each of you can find another husband to take care of you."

Ruth and Orpah loved Naomi so much that they wanted to journey with her to Judah. "We'll go with you," they both said.

"But I can't take care of you," Naomi insisted. "I have no money, no home, no land, no food."

The women cried and hugged. Naomi loved Orpah and Ruth. And Orpah and Ruth loved their mother-in-law.

What do you think you would have done? Would you rather be poor and hungry in your own country with your own family? Or would you rather be poor and hungry in a strange country?

Even though Orpah loved her mother-in-law, she chose to go back to Moab. Orpah kissed Naomi goodbye.

But Ruth still wanted to go with Naomi. Ruth told Naomi, "Where you go, I will go. Where you stay, I will stay. Your people will be my people. And your God will be my God."

You see, the people in Moab worshipped false gods. They didn't worship the one true God. Ruth chose Naomi. And Ruth chose the real God.

So the two women made the long journey back to Bethlehem. Bethlehem was now their home.

Now, Naomi and Ruth knew that God had made a rule. At harvest time, Israelite farmers should leave extra grain and crops in their fields. This was so that poor people could collect this leftover food. Ruth said, "Let me go to the fields and pick up leftover grain." And so Ruth went to work, gathering food for the two women to eat.

As part of God's plan, Ruth picked up grain in the field of a man named Boaz. Boaz was a very kind relative of Elimelek, who had been Naomi's husband.

Boaz asked his workers about the new woman picking up grain. They told him all about Ruth's kindness to Naomi. Generous Boaz told Ruth to collect as much food as she and Naomi needed each day. "Come back every day and collect more," he said.

Ruth couldn't wait to get home and tell Naomi what had happened. When Ruth told her about the kindness of Boaz and showed her all the grain she'd gathered, Naomi said, "Boaz is our redeemer."

Just like God had rules about leaving food for the poor, God also had rules for male relatives to take care of widows in the family and other women who needed help.

The special name for a family member who took care of a woman this way was called a *redeemer*. That's because the person usually redeems the land that once belonged to their relative. *Redeem* means "to buy back."

Kind Boaz offered to buy back the land that had once belonged to Elimelek, in order to clear the debt that Naomi owed. And he offered to marry Ruth and take care of both women.

Boaz was a generous and kind man with a big heart. He loved Naomi and Ruth dearly and took care of them.

Reflection

- God loves when we treat others kindly, especially those who are sad or can't take care of themselves.

- How can you show kindness to someone tomorrow?

- In the days of Naomi and Ruth, God had a plan for a redeemer to care for a family member. That was part of God's plan to show us that he would one day send his Son, Jesus, to be our redeemer, to pay the debt for our sins.

Prayer

Dear God, help me show kindness to everyone in my family. Help me show kindness to my friends. Help me be kind to my teachers, coaches, neighbors, and grocery store workers. Teach me to be kind to everybody I meet.

And, God, especially help me find ways to be kind to the poor and hungry and needy. Show me the best way to help them. Amen.

God Answers Hannah's Prayer

1 SAMUEL 1–3

A woman named Hannah was very sad. She loved her husband, Elkanah, and she loved God. But Hannah often cried because she had no children. She dearly wanted a child.

As was the custom in those days, Hannah and Elkanah made a journey once each year to a place called Shiloh. They brought their offerings to God and prayed at God's *tabernacle* there. The tabernacle was a tent so large that it was like a church building. The tabernacle in Shiloh was *so* far away from where Hannah and Elkanah lived that it took them a long time to get there.

How would you like to travel several days to get to church? Aren't we glad we don't have to travel that far to worship the Lord?

Every year, the trip made Hannah sad because it reminded her that God had not chosen to give her a child. Hannah cried each year, and she never stopped asking God for a child.

One year, during the trip, Hannah was especially sad. She cried, and she prayed and prayed. She begged God for a baby of her own. Tears streamed down her face as she asked God for a child. She prayed silently, in her heart, but her lips moved as if she were talking out loud.

Hannah prayed, *God, will you please remember me and give me a son? If I may only have a son, I will return him to you. He will serve you all the days of his life.*

Hannah was so distraught that she didn't even see Eli, the priest, standing nearby. Eli asked Hannah if she was not feeling well.

"I am deeply troubled and sad," Hannah told the priest. "I pray with tears for something that I want desperately."

Eli spoke words of comfort to Hannah and said a blessing for her. He said, "May God grant you what you have asked of him."

Eli's words made Hannah feel better. She stopped crying and felt peace in her heart.

God did hear Hannah, and he answered her prayer. Hannah gave birth to a precious little boy. She named him *Samuel* because the name meant "I asked the Lord for him."

Hannah loved Samuel very much and took good care of him. Even though she wished he could live with her forever, she remembered her promise to God. When Samuel was older, she journeyed again with her husband to Shiloh and took Samuel with her.

Hannah presented little Samuel to Eli, the priest. Hannah said, "Remember me? I'm the woman who stood here beside you and prayed to the Lord. I prayed for this child. God

answered my prayer. And now I give him to the Lord to serve God all the days of his life."

Hannah loved Samuel deeply. Leaving him with Eli in Shiloh made her sad, but she knew God wanted her son to be his special servant. She also knew Eli would take good care of Samuel, and she knew Samuel could serve God, even though he was a young boy.

Eli helped Samuel find ways to serve God at the tabernacle.

Hannah had kept her promise by taking Samuel to the tabernacle to live with Eli and serve God. And so God blessed Hannah and Elkanah with three more sons and two daughters.

Each year, when the family returned to the tabernacle to bring their sacrifices and offerings, Hannah brought a new robe for Samuel that she'd made with her own hands.

Young Samuel served the Lord every day in the tabernacle. Some of the people who came to the tabernacle might have wondered, *How can such a young boy serve the Lord?*

Even young kids can find ways to serve God!

Samuel kept working for the Lord and learning more about God every day. When Samuel was older, he became a mighty prophet for God. A *prophet* is a person who is a messenger for God. God speaks into the prophet's heart, and the prophet shares God's messages with the people.

Samuel often reminded the people of Israel to love and obey their loving God.

Reflection

- God loves us so much, and he listens to every one of our prayers. Sometimes, it may feel like God doesn't hear us if we don't get what we pray for. Since God knows what is best for us, sometimes his answer to our prayer request is "no." Sometimes his answer is "not now." And sometimes his answer is "yes."

- Can you name a recent "yes" from God?

- What about a "no"?

Prayer

Dear God, thank you for listening to every one of my prayers. Help me remember that even if I don't get exactly what I pray for, you know what is best for me.

Thank you that your answers to my prayers are always part of your plan for me. I love you, God. Amen.

Saul Becomes King

1 SAMUEL 8:1–13:14

Samuel, the prophet, led God's people for many years. When Samuel was an old man, the people of Israel asked for a king to lead them. They knew other nations had kings for leaders, and they wanted to be like the other nations.

God wanted to be the king of his chosen people. Remember, God had picked the people of Israel to be his chosen people.

The people begged and begged for a human king. God told Samuel to give the people what they wanted. But he also told Samuel to remind the Israelites that it was not a good idea to have a human king for a leader.

God loved his people very much, and he wanted what was best for them. God knew he was a wiser and more loving leader than a human king could ever be.

God loves you and me the same way too, and he wants what's best for us.

Have you ever wanted something really, really badly, but then when you got what you wanted, it wasn't a good thing? God didn't want that to happen to his people.

Nevertheless, he promised to reveal the man that Samuel should *anoint* as king.

What does it mean to anoint? Back in those days, a prophet or priest poured certain oils over a person's head to show that they had been chosen by God to do a special job. That is anointing.

Here's the funny way Samuel knew how to find the king. God told Samuel, "The man looking for his father's missing donkeys will be Israel's first king." That's an odd clue, right?

But Samuel met a man named Saul who was, indeed, looking for his father's missing donkeys. When Samuel anointed Saul, he said, "God has chosen you to be Israel's king."

Saul knew that would be a big job. At first, he didn't think he could do it. He said, "I come from the smallest tribe of Israel." Saul thought he was nobody important. Maybe that's part of the reason God chose Saul—because Saul was humble rather than proud.

When the time came for Samuel to tell all the people who would be king, Saul was nowhere to be found! Saul was so nervous about being king that he tried to hide! He thought he could hide from God and from the people.

Have you ever been so afraid of doing something that you hid under your bed or inside your closet? Hiding doesn't solve the problem, though.

God knew right where Saul was hiding, so he told the people, and they went and got Saul.

Saul must not have picked a very good hiding spot, right? Do you suppose he was a terrible hide-and-seek player? Maybe that's why he couldn't find his father's donkeys too, huh?

When Samuel presented Saul to the people of God, Samuel said, "Here's the man God chose to be your king. There is no one like him anywhere."

The people were happy because they got what they wanted. "Long live the king!" the people shouted.

Samuel wrote down everything God said about being a king, so that Saul would know how to be a good king.

Samuel warned the people again. First he said, "Fear the Lord." (To *fear* God means make sure you treat God as holy and perfect and good.) Then Samuel said, "If you serve and obey God, your nation will be blessed. If you rebel against God, he will not bless you."

At first, Saul was a very good king. He listened to God and did everything God told him to do. He rescued the Israelites from their enemies.

However, in a short time, Saul became filled with pride. He thought too highly of himself. Saul thought he'd won the battles and that he was a great king. He didn't give God praise or thanks for winning the battles. And he didn't obey God.

Samuel reminded Saul that God had expected obedience. He told Saul that God was going to take away his job as king because Saul didn't respect God.

Saul's pride had caused him to lose his job as king.

Reflection

- At first, King Saul obeyed God. Unfortunately, Saul's heart soon filled with pride. Instead of praising and thanking God for Israel's victories, Saul thought he deserved the praise himself.

- God wants us to give him praise for everything, since he blesses us with our abilities and successes.

- Do you sometimes struggle with pride?

- How can you change that?

- God doesn't want our hearts filled with pride. God wants our hearts filled with love for him.

Prayer

Dear God, sometimes I forget to give you praise and thanks for everything. At times, I can be prideful and think that I'm doing great things, like scoring goals or getting good test grades or running faster than my friends. Remind me that you are the one who helps me do all those things.

Help me to give you praise and thanks for all those good things. Please keep pride out of my heart. Amen.

David Trusts God

When King Saul no longer obeyed God, God told Samuel to anoint a new king. God sent Samuel to the family of a man named Jesse. God said, "One of Jesse's sons will be the new king."

Jesse lived in Bethlehem and had lots of sons. Jesse presented the sons to Samuel, beginning with the oldest son.

Samuel thought for sure that God wanted the oldest son. Samuel thought he looked like a king and had lived long enough to know how to be a good king.

"Nope, that's not the one," God said to Samuel. God reminded Samuel that the outside wasn't as important as the inside. God said, "People think about what a person looks like on the outside. But the Lord looks at the heart."

Jesse brought another son to Samuel.

God said, "Not that one either."

Another son, then another, and then another. Samuel watched seven of Jesse's sons pass by him. Each time, God said, "Not that one."

Samuel had just about given up, thinking that was all the sons. He asked Jesse, "Do you have any other sons?"

Jesse said, "The youngest is out tending sheep."

Later, when David came home from tending the sheep, Samuel might have thought, *You're kidding, right, God?* But Samuel was surprised to hear God say, "This is the one." Samuel didn't expect God to choose the youngest son. Even though David was handsome and strong, Samuel had thought God would pick a different son.

God doesn't want us to make decisions about people by just looking at their outside appearance. When we do that, we're judging other people. God wants us to get to know the person's heart—what they're like on the inside.

Once Samuel anointed David, David went back to work in the fields with his father's flocks. It wasn't time for him to become king yet. For now, David's job was to tend the sheep.

David worked hard to protect his father's flocks. He protected the sheep from bears and lions. He was a good shepherd. David trusted God to help him take care of the sheep. And he trusted God to one day help him be a good king.

Besides being a good shepherd, David was a good musician too. He played the harp beautifully. He played so well that many people knew about his skills. Someone asked him to come play the harp for King Saul. When King Saul had a bad day and became angry, David's music calmed him.

David's older brothers were part of King Saul's army. They helped defend the Israelites against the enemies of God's

people. One group of people, the Philistines, gave the children of God a lot of trouble. They picked fights often and took things from the Israelites.

Once, when King Saul's army and the Philistine army were fighting, David's father asked David to go to the battlefield and check on his older brothers. David's father, Jesse, gave him bread and other food to take to his brothers.

When David got there, he saw a really tall man in the Philistine army who looked like a giant. Everyone was afraid of the giant, whose name was Goliath. But David wanted to fight Goliath. David wanted to help the people of Israel.

King Saul told him, "You're not able to fight this giant. You are just a young man. A shepherd."

But David told the king that he'd fought lions and bears while tending his father's sheep. David said, "God will rescue me from the Philistine." David trusted God to help him defeat Goliath.

King Saul offered his armor to David, but it was too big for the young man. Instead, David picked up five smooth stones and put them in a pouch. He bravely walked up to the giant with just those five stones and a slingshot.

David aimed a rock at Goliath with his slingshot. Just one smooth stone took down the bully giant. The frightened Philistine army turned and ran away.

God's people were safe once more because David had trusted God to help him.

Reflection

- David trusted God when he found out he would one day be king. And when he played the harp for a king. And when he had to fight a giant.

- David had practiced trusting God ever since he was a little boy. All that practicing made it easier for David to trust God when he fought a giant.

- How can you practice trusting God?

- What can you trust God to help you with tomorrow?

Prayer

Dear God, please lead me to trust you, like David did. Help me trust you with little things every day, so that I can also trust you with big things.

And, God, I may not have to fight a giant like David did, but please help me trust you when I feel like I am under attack by people who don't love you. Amen.

David Is a Good Friend

King Saul celebrated the victory that they had won over the bully giant and the Philistine army. He was happy that David had brought peace to the people of Israel. He asked David to move into the king's home. He wanted David to be like family.

King Saul also sent David on a lot of military missions. God made sure that David always succeeded.

While living in the king's home, David became best friends with the king's son, Jonathan. They spent time together. Jonathan gave David his royal robe, sword, and bow. They were kind to each other.

Saul delighted in David's company and his victories in battle . . . at first. But before long, the people of Israel began to praise David for all his victories. The people praised David even more than they praised Saul.

The king's nasty pride got in the way again! He didn't like David getting all the attention. He grew angrier and angrier. One day, King Saul got so angry that he threw his spear at David. The king wanted to hurt him.

Sounds pretty dangerous to live in the king's palace, right? The king's temper was *really* bad!

David escaped the flying spear—twice—but Saul was so angry that he sent David out on many battles. He secretly hoped the Philistine army would kill David. King Saul was so jealous of David that he even asked his son, Jonathan, and his servants to kill David.

Best friends David and Jonathan were sad that King Saul was so jealous and angry. The two friends wanted to help each other. Jonathan warned David to beware of King Saul's anger. Jonathan begged his father not to harm David. He spoke highly of his friend to King Saul.

Saul promised not to harm David. And he kept his promise . . . but not for long. After David came back from another battle, King Saul threatened him again with a spear.

King Saul probably should have practiced controlling his anger instead of practicing throwing spears, right?

This time, David knew he was no longer safe with King Saul.

Jonathan said, "Let us test my father's anger. He has invited you to a big dinner, which is coming up soon. Don't go to his dinner. On the evening after it, go and hide in the field. I'll shoot three arrows. If King Saul, my father, really wants to harm you, I will say to my servant, 'Look, the arrows are beyond you.'"

Well, sure enough, King Saul's anger raged the night of the big dinner because David didn't show up. Jonathan shot

the three arrows and gave David the secret message to flee as quickly as possible.

Jonathan and David met one last time to say goodbye. The two hugged and cried. They were sad to say goodbye because they loved each other as best friends. They promised to always be friends. The young men treated each other kindly, just the way friends should treat one another.

When good friends care for each other, they keep their promises. Many years later, after David became king, he wanted to honor his promise to his good friend, Jonathan. David had promised to take care of Jonathan's family. King David asked his servants to find any member of Jonathan's family still living nearby, so he could care for them.

Jonathan had one son left named Mephibosheth. Mephibosheth had two hurt feet and couldn't take care of himself very well. King David invited Mephibosheth to come to the palace and live there forever. He promised to take care of him. And he gave Mephibosheth back all the land that had belonged to his grandfather, King Saul. It was King David's way of honoring his friend, Jonathan.

Mephibosheth was very grateful to King David. He moved to the palace. He sat with the king every night for dinner. That made both of the men very happy. And no more flying spears!

Reflection

- Jonathan and David loved each other as best friends. They never forgot each other.

- The two friends show us how God wants us to treat our friends. God wants us to treat others with kindness and loyalty. When we treat our friends with kindness, we show the world that we love God and want to be obedient to him.

- In what ways can you show kindness to your friends?

- How will you do that tomorrow?

Prayer

Dear God, thank you for Bible stories like this one that teach me how to be a good friend. Please lead me to be kind to my friends. Lead me to share with my friends and to help them when they need help.

Thank you, God, for being my friend. I love you. Amen.

Solomon, a Wise King

2 SAMUEL 5–7; 1 KINGS 1–8

David was a good king who loved the Lord. He worked hard to take care of God's people. He often talked to God in prayer, and he wrote songs about God too. Even though he was a good king who usually put God first, David made some bad choices and mistakes. Those made God sad. Each time David sinned, he realized it and then prayed and asked God to forgive him.

God wants us to ask for forgiveness when we do wrong too. Like David, we can stop sinning and ask God to forgive us.

David went to battle and took back the beautiful city of Jerusalem for God's people. The Israelites danced and celebrated. David gave Jerusalem a new name, the City of David.

King David decided to have a large, fancy palace built there. Kings from other countries sent supplies to King David for his palace. They were David's friends, and they wanted to give him good gifts. It took many years for the palace to be completed.

Later, David felt sad that he had an amazing palace to live in, but God's special chest, the ark of the covenant, still sat in a tent. David wanted to build a grand *temple*—a church—for God and his ark of the covenant. David told one of God's great prophets, Nathan, about his plan to build a temple. At first, Nathan thought it was a great idea too.

But that very night, God spoke to Nathan. God told Nathan that one of David's sons would build God's temple.

Nathan told King David what God had said.

Even though David knew he wouldn't be the king to build a house for God, he made plans for the temple and gathered supplies.

When David was too old to be king any longer, some of his sons argued over who would be king next. But God wanted David's son Solomon to be king.

David obeyed God and gave Solomon the job of being the next king. David reminded Solomon to make sure the Israelite people worshipped only God.

David also gave his son some good advice about being king. He told him to always follow God, so that the job of king could stay in their family.

Solomon knew that he had a lot to learn about being the king. One night, God appeared to Solomon in a dream. God told him he could ask for anything. What Solomon wanted most of all was to be a good king for God's people. So, in the dream, Solomon asked God for *wisdom*. He wanted to know right from wrong.

What would you have asked for?

Would you rather have wisdom or wealth?

Would you rather have good looks or be kind?

Would you rather have a huge palace or a smaller home with kind and loving people?

God was pleased that Solomon had asked for wisdom. God knew that Solomon could have asked for money or many other things, but instead, he'd asked for wisdom.

In the dream, God told Solomon that because he'd asked for wisdom, God would make him one of the wisest people who ever lived. That way, Solomon could take good care of God's chosen people.

Solomon did rule the people wisely. He made many good decisions and wrote amazing songs and *proverbs*. Proverbs are wise sayings.

Solomon also collected supplies for the temple, like his father, David, had done. Solomon picked just the right builders and workers.

Lots of people had different jobs to do for the temple. God gave each person special talents to do their job well.

When the temple had been built, Solomon and the leaders of Israel placed God's ark of the covenant in the temple. As soon as the priests stepped away from the ark, God's tall cloud, the one the Israelites had followed in the desert for 40 years, filled the temple.

God's cloud showed Solomon and the people of Israel—as well as people from other countries—that God was personally taking care of his people.

Reflection

- What special talent or gift do you feel like God has given you?

- How can you use that talent to serve God?

- Solomon used God's gift of wisdom to serve God. God wants us to ask for wisdom too. We can ask God to help us know the difference between right and wrong.

- We can also ask God for the wisdom to treat other people fairly and kindly.

Prayer

Dear God, thank you for this story that reminds me to ask for wisdom. Thank you that I can ask for wisdom about anything. I can ask you to help me spell words correctly on my test. I can ask you to give me wisdom to eat the right foods. I can ask for wisdom when playing with my friends. I can ask for wisdom to make right choices.

Help me be wise, God. Amen.

Elijah in the Wilderness

1 KINGS 17–18

Lots of different kings ruled in Israel and in Judah over the years. Some of the kings remembered God and worshipped only him. But many of the kings turned away from God.

After a long time, a man named Ahab became king of Israel. He did not worship the one true God. And his wife, Jezebel? Well, let's just say she was not a nice person at all. She was so cruel that she wanted a lot of people dead! She worshipped the false god Baal. Ahab and Jezebel led God's people to disobey God.

God was unhappy with the people of Israel. He gave a message to one of his prophets, a good man named Elijah.

Then Elijah took God's message to King Ahab. Elijah said, "In God's name, I tell you that no rain will fall on the land in the next few years."

The king knew that the people would have no food to eat if rain didn't fall. This made King Ahab and Queen Jezebel angry.

God knew they would be angry with Elijah, so God told Elijah to hide in the wilderness. God sent ravens to Elijah every day with bread and meat for Elijah to eat.

Kind of like pizza-delivery guys.

What would you think about birds bringing you breakfast and dinner every day? Sounds really neat, huh? If you could pick any animal in the world to bring you food every day, which animal would you pick?

Elijah hid in the wilderness, next to a stream of water, for quite some time. But then the lack of rainfall caused the brook near Elijah to dry up. God told Elijah to go to the city of Zarephath next. God told him to look for a certain woman there who would give him food.

Elijah found the woman, a widow, at Zarephath and asked for some water to drink and bread to eat.

She told Elijah, "I have no food to offer you. The famine is severe. I only have enough flour and oil to make one more meal for my son and me, and then we'll have no more food."

Imagine her surprise when Elijah told her that God promised to make sure she had enough food to last until the rain came again! Elijah said, "God says your jar of flour will not run out, nor will your jug of oil run dry."

The woman trusted the words that God had spoken through Elijah. She prepared a meal for the three of them. Because God's words are always true, the widow, her son, and Elijah had enough food every day. God made sure the jar of flour and jug of oil never ran out.

After a long time with no rain, Elijah told King Ahab to meet him at the top of Mount Carmel. Elijah wanted to prove to all the people that God is the only true God.

On top of the mountain, Elijah challenged the king and the prophets of the false god Baal. Elijah said, "If you think your Baal god is real, follow him. But if the Lord is God, follow him."

Elijah instructed the king's false prophets to build an altar to their fake god. Meanwhile, Elijah built an altar to the Lord. Then Elijah told King Ahab's prophets, "Call on your god, Baal, to light his altar fire." While all the people watched, nothing happened.

Elijah even taunted the people. "Maybe your god is deep in thought or traveling. Maybe he is asleep."

Perhaps Elijah was practicing to be a stand-up comedian, because he knew the one true God never, ever sleeps!

Despite shouts and noise by the people, nothing happened to their false god's altar.

Then Elijah prayed out loud, "Lord, God of Abraham, Isaac, and Israel, let everyone know today that you are God in Israel. Answer me, Lord, so that all these people will know you are God, so they will come back to you."

Immediately fire fell from the sky, and flames burned on the Lord's altar.

The Israelites believed in God again. Elijah told everyone that rain was on the way.

The people must have thought that was part of the comedy show too, because there wasn't a cloud in the sky! After Elijah's servant had checked the sky eight times, he told Elijah, "I think I see a small cloud."

Sure enough, that small cloud soon turned into a huge rain. The people would have crops and food once again!

Reflection

- When people turn their hearts away from God, things go wrong.

- God gets sad when people forget him and choose other things first.

- Are there things more important to you than God? Do you watch too much television and forget to pray? Do you want too many toys and forget to give some of your money back to God at church?

- What can you do to turn your heart or actions back to God?

Prayer

Dear God, I'm sorry when I love other things more than you. Please help me to love you the most—not my toys, games, television, schoolwork, or even my family and friends! Help me remember to worship only you because you are the one true God.

Thank you for loving me, even when I do wrong. I love you so much, God! Amen.

Elisha Helps a Widow

1 KINGS 19:19–21; 2 KINGS 2:1–18; 4:1–7

For years, Elijah, the prophet, worked hard for God and did good things for God's people. He told them God's messages and encouraged them to worship only God.

God took care of Elijah and provided for him all those years. (Remember the ravens that brought him bread and meat, like pizza-delivery guys?) When Elijah grew old, God told him to find a man named Elisha to take over the work of God.

Elijah went in search of Elisha.

Those two names sound a lot alike, don't they? One easy way to remember which prophet had the job first is this: The letter "j" comes before the letter "s" in the alphabet. So, Elijah with a "j" came before Elisha with an "s." Super easy now, right?

Elijah found Elisha working in the field, plowing. Elijah said, "God has chosen you to be his prophet." He might have even told him, "You'll get to do some really cool things for God. But some people might not like you because you'll need to point out their sins. And there just might be a wicked-lady queen who wants you dead. And you might be fed by ravens one day. And you might get to hold back the rain and cause a famine and then call down fire from heaven. It's a *really* cool job!"

Elijah probably didn't say all those exact words. However, Elijah had certainly lived a wild and adventurous life as God's prophet.

Elisha was ready to do God's work. He probably wiped the dirt off his hands from working in the field and shook Elijah's hand. His one request was to say goodbye to his father and mother before they left.

Which job do you think you'd like best? Working in a garden or sharing God's messages? Maybe you could even find a way to do both!

Elisha spent time with Elijah, learning as much as he could about God's work. By now, Elijah was very old. He knew he would soon go to heaven to be with God.

One day, while Elijah and Elisha were walking together, Elijah took off his cloak, rolled it up like a scroll, and struck the Jordan River. The waters parted, and the two men walked across on dry ground. On the other side of the river, Elijah asked Elisha, "What can I do for you before I leave you?"

Elisha said, "I want to have a double portion of your spirit." Elisha wanted to serve God in spectacular ways, just like Elijah had served him.

While they were talking, horses of fire and a chariot of fire suddenly appeared, along with a whirling wind. Elijah stepped onto the chariot, and then the horses took him away to heaven.

That's quite an exit, right?

Elisha was sad that his friend, teacher, and mighty man of God was gone. Elisha spotted Elijah's cloak on the ground. When Elisha struck the Jordan River with the cloak, the waters parted, just like they had for Elijah. Elisha knew it was time for him to carry on the work of God.

A widow needed help from Elisha. Because she had no job, she couldn't pay her debts. She told Elisha she only had a little bit of oil left in her home.

Elisha had great compassion on the poor woman and her hungry sons. He said, "Go to your neighbors' houses. Borrow empty jars. Ask for lots of jars! Then go inside your house. Let your sons help you pour the oil into the jars. Keep pouring until every jar is full."

The widow must have wondered, *Didn't Elisha just hear me say that I only had a little bit of oil left? Why do I need so many jars?* She might have thought those words, but she didn't say them. She believed in God and knew he was a god of miracles. She trusted and believed that God would take care of her and her sons. She did just what Elisha told her to do.

The little bit of oil filled lots and lots of jars. Then she took the jars to the market to sell the oil. She used the money to pay her debts and buy food. Now the widow could provide for her sons.

God had helped the widow through his new prophet, Elisha.

Reflection

- God called Elisha to be his prophet. Elisha happily served the Lord. He tried extra hard to learn everything he needed to know from Elijah so he would do a good job.

- When you do something for God, do you work extra hard to serve God well? Do you give God your best?

- And do you love God's people like Elisha did?

- Elisha felt compassion for the poor widow. Have you ever helped someone in need?

Prayer

Dear God, I want to serve you well, like Elisha did. Help me read and study your words in the Bible so I know how to do that. Lead me to talk to you often in prayer. Show me how to help people in need. Amen.

The Bold, Young Servant Girl

2 KINGS 5:1–16

Once, soldiers from the country of Aram snuck into Israel. The soldiers took things that didn't belong to them. They even stole some of the people living there!

One young Israelite girl was snatched by the soldiers. She became a servant in Aram. She worked in the house of a man named Naaman, taking care of Naaman's wife.

Naaman was a great warrior in Aram. He won lots of battles, which made the king of Aram happy. But Naaman had a problem. The mighty fighter had a disease called *leprosy*. Leprosy caused sores all over Naaman's body. Ouch! Painful scabs covered his arms and legs.

The servant girl from Israel saw the sores and wanted to help Naaman. She knew God could heal him.

Even though she was far from home and missed her family, she remembered that her family served God and worshipped him. She also remembered Elisha, God's prophet in Israel.

One day, the servant girl spoke boldly. She told Naaman's wife that Naaman should go see the prophet Elisha. "He will cure my master of leprosy," the girl said.

Naaman told the king about the young girl's words.

"Go to Israel," the king of Aram said. He wrote a letter for Naaman to take to the king of Israel. The letter said, "Here is my chief soldier, Naaman, so that you may cure him of leprosy." Naaman's king gave him gifts to take to the king of Israel.

Naaman and some of his servants traveled to Israel.

When the king of Israel read the letter, he was stunned. He tore his clothes in fear. "How can I heal this man?" the king of Israel asked. "The king of Aram wants to pick a fight with me!"

When the prophet Elisha heard that the king had torn his clothes in a panic, the man of God sent a message to the king. "Send the man to me," Elisha said. "I will heal him. Then he'll know there is a true prophet living in Israel."

Horses and chariots thundered to Elisha's house, carrying Naaman and his servants.

Elisha did not come outside to see Naaman. He sent a messenger instead. The messenger told Naaman, "Go wash in the Jordan River seven times, and your skin will be healed."

The mighty warrior stomped around in anger. "Why didn't the prophet come out and speak to me?" Naaman yelled. "I thought he would call on the name of the Lord and wave his hands over my sores to make them go away."

Naaman complained to his servants. "Surely the rivers in Aram are better than the waters here in Israel." He stomped all the way back to his chariot.

Naaman's servants begged him to listen to Elisha. One gently said, "If the man of God had told you to do something hard, wouldn't you do it? How much easier it is for you to simply wash in the river." The servants talked Naaman into obeying the prophet.

Naaman walked into the river. He dunked himself until water covered the sores on his body.

One dunk in the water.

Two dunks.

Three dunks.

Four, five, six dunks.

Seven dunks.

Naaman washed seven times in the Jordan River, just like the man of God had said. And his skin was healed.

"I'm clean!" Naaman may have shouted. "I'm cured! My scabs are gone."

Still dripping wet, Naaman looked at his arms and legs and smiled because they looked as healthy as a young boy's. He might have even thought that they looked as healthy as the arms of the young servant girl who had suggested that he go and see Elisha.

Naaman returned with his servants to the house of Elisha. This time, Naaman shouted with joy! "Now I know that there is no God in all the world except in Israel," Naaman told Elisha.

When Naaman tried to give Elisha gifts, Elisha wouldn't take them.

Soon after, Naaman began his journey home, with his skin completely healed.

The servant girl's bold words about the man of God had helped Naaman. Her courage and thoughtfulness helped him find a cure for his sores.

And her words had helped Naaman to learn about God.

Reflection

- Despite being a servant, the young girl treated her masters with such kindness that she could speak boldly about God.

- And so God had used the young servant girl in a big way.

- Have you told anyone about God recently?

- Have you told anyone these Bible stories you've been reading about God?

- How can you trust God to help you to tell people about him?

Prayer

Dear God, please help me be kind to others, even when I might not feel like being kind and even when they haven't been kind to me.

Help me have compassion on people who are sick or have needs.

And most especially, please help me be bold and tell others about you and how much you love everybody. Amen.

Isaiah, a Special Prophet

ISAIAH 6; 9:1-7

God's chosen people drifted farther and farther from God during the reign of kings. Most of the kings didn't follow God, so their people didn't follow God. The kings led the people to do bad things.

God had chosen Abraham's descendants—his children's children's children—to be his special people. God wanted them to show the world how to live the right way.

He'd told them over and over again to follow only him. God promised to protect them *if* they followed him. But God warned the people what would happen if they didn't follow him.

"If you don't follow and obey me, I will punish you," he said.

Do you think that got their attention? Nope. The people didn't listen. They kept doing bad things.

They couldn't even get along with each other. When they hadn't been able to agree about which new king to choose, the people had split the nation into two countries—Israel in the north and Judah in the south. Then they each had their own king.

Still, God never gave up on his special people. He promised to always love them. Their sin angered God, but he kept loving them.

Time after time, God warned the people to follow him. Here's how he did it. God called some of his faithful people to be prophets. Remember, a prophet is a messenger. God asked these prophets to share his messages with the people.

Sometimes, being a prophet was a scary job. Why? Because most of the time, the people didn't want to hear God's messages from the prophets. And the people would get angry when the prophets scolded them for not obeying God. The people didn't like hearing that God would punish them if they didn't change their ways.

Could you do that job? Could you be bold enough to share God's words, even if you knew it might make people angry?

One of God's special prophets was a man named Isaiah. Isaiah had a *vision* about God. A vision is like a dream where God really talks to you. In the vision that God gave to Isaiah, Isaiah saw God sitting on his throne. God's robe was magnificent. It filled the whole temple.

Isaiah saw two creatures with wings above God, called "seraphim." The two seraphim said, "Holy, holy, holy is the Lord Almighty. The whole earth is full of his glory."

The temple rattled and shook when the seraphim spoke. Smoke filled the temple.

Isaiah realized he was in the presence of God. He didn't feel worthy to be there. "I am a sinful man!" he said. "Everything I say is sinful!"

One of the winged creatures used tongs to lift a hot coal from the altar. The seraphim flew to Isaiah, touched Isaiah's lips with the hot coal, and said, "Your sin is taken away. You are no longer guilty."

Then Isaiah heard God say, "Whom shall I send? Who will go speak to the people?"

Isaiah said, "Here am I. Send me!"

Isaiah wanted to be God's prophet. He wanted to speak God's messages to the Israelites.

Soon, the vision ended.

Before long, other countries invaded Israel and Judah. The armies took many of the people far away as prisoners. Isaiah told them God's messages. He said God would bring them back to their homeland one day. He told the people to keep believing in God and to stay strong.

God also gave Isaiah a really important message to share with his people. It was the greatest message of hope that Isaiah ever shared. A message of hope for the whole world.

Isaiah said, "God will send a *Savior*. This Savior will come to earth to save the whole world from their sins. He will redeem—bring to himself—every person who believes in him. He will be the greatest King, but his home won't be a palace. He'll be a healer and a rescuer and a servant. Many people won't like him, but he will love the entire world.

"And he will be called 'Wonderful Counselor, Mighty God, Everlasting Father, Prince of Peace.'"

Isaiah shared this great and beautiful promise of hope for the Israelites and the whole world.

He was talking about God's Son.

Jesus.

Reflection

- God's people stopped loving God, but God never stopped loving them.

- He sent prophets to tell the people to repent. That means to turn away from sin and turn back to God.

- Do you think it would be hard to give someone a message they didn't want to hear?

- Isaiah kept telling people about God, even though they didn't want to hear Isaiah's words. He even offered them hope.

- Could you be that bold?

Prayer

Dear God, it's hard to believe that people turned their backs on you in Bible days. But when I sin and break your rules, I'm turning my back on you too. When I skip prayer time and put me first, I'm forgetting you, just like they did. I'm sorry, God.

Thank you for loving me, even when I mess up. Amen.

Jonah's Big Fish Story

JONAH 1–3

Prophets in the Bible spoke God's messages to his people. God gave messages to the prophets, and the prophets gave the messages to the people.

"Turn from your evil ways." That's what the prophets told God's people. God wanted the people to repent, to turn away from their sins. He hoped they would listen to the prophets.

One day, God spoke to one of his prophets, a man named Jonah. God said, "Jonah, go to the great city of Nineveh."

Jonah might have said, "Whoa, wait. Hold up."

You see, Nineveh was a huge city in Assyria. That country was an enemy of the Israelites. Jonah didn't want to go there to give God's message.

God told Jonah, "Go to Nineveh and tell the people to turn from their wicked ways."

Instead of going to Nineveh, Jonah ran away from God. Jonah thought, *I'll get on this ship and sail in the opposite direction.* The ship sailed with Jonah on board.

Well, that doesn't sound like a smart plan at all, right? No one, nobody, not one single person can run away from God.

Guess what God did? God sent a great wind and storm. Giant waves tossed that ship around like it was a toy. The sailors thought for sure they were going to perish! They threw some of the cargo overboard, hoping to save the ship.

Somehow, Jonah managed to fall asleep during the violent storm. One of the sailors finally woke up Jonah and said, "Pray to your God to save us."

You see, the other sailors had already prayed to their false gods, but no one had prayed to the one true God.

Jonah told the sailors, "This storm is my fault. I tried to run away from God. I worship the Lord, the God of heaven, who made the sea and the dry land."

The sailors were likely wishing for some dry land!

Jonah told the men to throw him overboard, and then the storm would stop.

The sailors didn't want to throw Jonah into the sea. Instead, they rowed harder and harder. They hoped to reach the shore.

Yet the winds roared more and more, and the sea swirled and splashed and foamed.

The men soon decided to toss Jonah overboard. They cried out to God, "Please, Lord, don't punish us for taking this man's life."

The sailors flung Jonah into the raging sea. *Splash,* went Jonah. The seas calmed, and the boat stopped rocking.

And then, as odd as it seems, God sent a big fish to swallow Jonah. Yep, swallowed him whole, right there in the water.

Jonah spent three whole days and nights in the stinky, gross belly of the fish.

Ew, now that's a smelly punishment, right? Would you rather be tossed about in a violent storm or swallowed by a fish? Tough choice, huh?

Guess what Jonah did? Besides hold his nose. Well, first, he probably realized running from God was a really dumb plan. Then, he prayed. Jonah asked God to forgive him for running away. He promised to do what God wanted.

After Jonah prayed, God caused the fish to spit Jonah out onto dry land. And Jonah headed straight to Nineveh!

Let's hope he found someplace to shower first. Otherwise, the people of Nineveh might say, "Something's fishy here, Jonah."

Jonah told all the people to repent. "Turn from your evil ways," he said. "Stop sinning, or God is going to destroy your city. Don't worship idols. Don't worship other gods. Worship the one true God."

The people of Nineveh listened to Jonah. They stopped sinning. The king repented too. The Ninevites turned from their evil ways and turned to God instead.

God was pleased and decided not to destroy the city.

Reflection

- Where is your best hiding spot for a hide-and-seek game?

- Have you ever felt like you could hide from God?

- There's no place we can hide from God—ever!

- Jonah found that out the hard way. God wanted Jonah to go to Nineveh because God loved those people too. God loved the whole world then, and he loves the whole world now. God wants everyone to know him and to know that he loves them.

Prayer

Dear God, help me remember that I can't run away from you, because you promise to be with me everywhere. You're with me at home, school, church, when I'm shopping, when I'm outside, when I'm on a boat or in an airplane. And if I manage to find myself in the belly of a fish, you'll be there too.

Thank you for loving the whole world. Help me love the world also. Amen.

The Fiery Furnace

DANIEL 1–3

God's people disobeyed and forgot him. So, just like he'd warned them he would do, God took his hand of protection away from his chosen people. The army of Babylon invaded Jerusalem. The soldiers took some of the Israelites back with them to be servants in Babylon.

The king of Babylon had a really long name. It was Nebuchadnezzar. Try saying that three times fast!

King Nebuchadnezzar told his chief official to pick some of the young, healthy men from Jerusalem to train in his court. They were to learn the Babylonian language and culture. The king wanted men who were smart, hardworking, good students. Four of the young men picked by the official were friends, and they loved and obeyed God. Their names were Daniel, Shadrach, Meshach, and Abednego.

These young men studied hard. But they never forgot God. Even though they had been taken from their homeland to another country that had fake gods, they remembered the one true God and worshipped only him.

The young men studied hard and learned so much that they received special jobs as advisors.

King Nebuchadnezzar and his armies became so powerful that they took over many lands. The king became quite proud of all his victories. His heart filled with such pride that he ordered some of his people to build a huge statue of himself. It was taller than 16 men and covered in gold. And if that wasn't bad enough, the king said everyone should bow down and worship the statue several times every day!

King Nebuchadnezzar told his messenger to tell people, "Whenever you hear the king's band play music, fall down on the ground and worship the golden image of the king." And guess what else he told them? "If you don't bow to the golden image, you'll be thrown into a blazing hot furnace of fire."

Whoa. That's pretty scary, right? What do you think Daniel's three friends did when they heard the music? Do you think Shadrach, Meshach, and Abednego worshipped the golden statue? What would you have done?

Well, you guessed it. The three men did *not* bow down or worship the statue. Shadrach, Meshach, and Abednego knew they could only worship God. Which worked fine, until some tattletales in the kingdom wanted to get them in trouble.

"King, King, King!" someone tattled. "Shadrach, Meshach, and Abednego aren't worshipping your statue."

This made the king angry. He called for the three men. "What's going on?" he might have said. "You heard the rule. Bow to my statue or go into the fire."

Do you think the young men's knees shook in fear? Do you think they broke out in a sweat, even though they weren't near the fire yet?

Nope. Not at all.

The bold, young men answered, "If we are thrown into the blazing fire, the God we serve can save us. But even if the Lord chooses not to save us, we cannot serve your gods. We will serve our God only."

How about you? Could you be that bold?

King Nebuchadnezzar burned with anger. (Get it? *Burned* with anger?) He told his soldiers to make the fire even hotter than before. Seven times hotter!

That's hot, right? Can you think of the hottest you've ever been? On a beach in the summer? On a school bus with no air conditioner? Try making that seven times hotter. Yikes!

The king's soldiers tied up the young men and threw them into the furnace.

Then the king looked into the furnace. He thought he'd see nothing but flames. To his surprise, he saw men walking around in the furnace.

But not three men—one, two, three, FOUR men. And no one was tied up!

God had sent the angel of the Lord to protect Shadrach, Meshach, and Abednego.

The king quickly called the men out of the furnace. Shadrach, Meshach, and Abednego walked out. They were unharmed. No burned clothes. No smoky smells. Not a hair on their heads was harmed.

The king said, "Now I know you worship the one true God."

Whew! Talk about being in the hot seat. Good thing the three men had trusted God!

Reflection

- Do you think it was hard for the three men to stand up to the king?

- Have you ever experienced a time when everyone around you did something wrong and you chose to do the right thing? Like, maybe your friends made fun of a new student and you didn't?

- Sometimes it's hard to be the only person doing the right thing. But that's just what God wants us to do.

Prayer

Dear God, help me be strong like Shadrach, Meshach, and Abednego and always choose to do the right thing . . . even if everyone around me chooses to do wrong.

Help me know that you will always be with me, that you'll always protect me. Amen.

Daniel in the Lions' Den

DANIEL 4 – 6

People all over Babylon likely heard about Shadrach, Meshach, Abednego, and that blazing hot furnace. So you'd think they'd learn not to tattle on God's people.

But that's not what happened.

Let's back up just a little.

Remember Daniel, the friend of Shadrach, Meshach, and Abednego? Daniel was smart and hardworking, just like his three friends. Daniel received a very important job in the palace of the king.

Because he listened to God, Daniel was so wise that the king once called him to interpret his dream. This success made the king like Daniel even more.

Later, Daniel interpreted another message from God. This time, the message was for King Nebuchadnezzar's son, Belshazzar. "You'll soon lose the kingdom," Daniel told King Belshazzar.

And just like that, King Belshazzar was no more. King Darius took over.

It's kind of hard to keep up with all the kings and kingdoms back then, right?

King Darius respected Daniel. Daniel impressed the king because Daniel was smart and worked hard. Even though he'd been taken from his own country, Daniel worked hard at everything he did. This made the king happy.

King Darius was so pleased that he planned to put Daniel in charge of the whole kingdom.

Well, this didn't go over too well with some of the other workers in King Darius' court. They were jealous of Daniel.

Do you ever get jealous of others? That happens sometimes to everyone. But God can take away our jealousy if we pray and ask him. And then, instead of feeling jealous, we can feel happy that God has blessed the other person, because God gives us special blessings too.

"Why should Daniel get that job?" one person might have asked.

"I want that job," another one could have grumbled.

"Let's set a trap for Daniel and get him in trouble," somebody decided.

The men knew Daniel was such a hard worker that they couldn't get him in trouble that way. They also knew he worshipped the one true God and prayed to him. How did they know that? They saw him praying while looking out his window toward Jerusalem. They watched him pray quietly to God three times every day.

The men tricked King Darius into signing a law. The law said that no one could pray to anyone except to King Darius for the next 30 days. And anyone who broke the law would be thrown into the lions' den.

The mean men watched Daniel and waited.

Do you think Daniel skipped his prayers for the next 30 days? Nope. Not Daniel.

So guess what the men did? Yep—they tattled.

"King, King, King!" said one of the men. "Daniel is praying to his God and not to you."

King Darius didn't want Daniel to be in trouble. He liked and respected Daniel. But the law was the law. He'd signed it himself.

The king was sad and said to Daniel, "May your God, whom you serve every day, rescue you!" The king hoped that would come true.

The king's men threw Daniel into the lions' den and rolled a stone over the mouth of the den. Because he had to, the king made sure the stone was sealed tight. Then he went back to his palace. He probably wished he'd never signed the law. He felt too sick to eat his dinner that night. He couldn't sleep either.

Early the next morning, the king hurried to the lions' den. The king yelled, "Daniel, has your God, the one you serve every day, rescued you?"

I'll bet the king's heart raced while he waited for an answer.

What do you think the king heard? Well, he didn't hear lions roaring. Do you know why?

Suddenly, a voice from the pit of lions said, "My God sent an angel, and he shut the mouths of the lions. I'm safe and unharmed."

The king was happy. Daniel was happy. And the lions might have been hungry.

King Darius told all the people about Daniel's amazing and powerful God.

Reflection

- What helps you remember to talk to God every day?

- Daniel was so committed to praying to God every day that he wasn't about to let a law stop him.

- Daniel trusted God to take care of him when he prayed three times every day.

- We can trust God to take care of us too.

Prayer

Dear God, I know it's unlikely that I'll ever be thrown into a lions' den for talking to you, but please help me to be as brave as Daniel, no matter what comes my way.

Help me to be faithful to you, like Daniel, and to serve and worship only you. Amen.

The Captives Go Home

EZRA 1; 3; 6:19–7:6; NEHEMIAH 2–3; 8–9; 12:43

"We're going home! We're going home!"

Just like God had promised, his chosen people were about to return to their homeland. King Cyrus had become king of Persia. He'd told God's people they were free to go back home to Israel. He even gave them silver and gold to take back with them. He instructed them to rebuild God's temple.

The people were thrilled to return to their own country. They gathered their families and started on their way.

When they arrived, the people found the city of Jerusalem and God's holy temple in ruins. Once they were settled in their homes, the people came together to sacrifice burnt offerings to the Lord. They celebrated God's festivals and brought other offerings to God. The people rejoiced that they were home again.

Soon, they got busy rebuilding the temple.

"Pass the hammers," said the carpenters.

"Bring the bricks," said the masons.

"Gather the cedar logs," said another worker.

The people worked and prayed and worked and worshipped.

When the last stone of the temple foundation found its place, the priests cheerfully sounded the trumpets and the Levites clanged the cymbals. The people sang praises to God and wept tears of joy.

Ezra, a great teacher of God's laws, reminded the people to always worship God.

A man named Nehemiah returned home from Babylon to help God's people rebuild the walls around Jerusalem. When the people had finished building the walls, Ezra read from the Book of the Law of God.

You see, many, many years had passed since the people had really worshipped God. They'd forgotten almost everything God had told them long ago. The people listened to the words that Ezra read, and they wept. They were ashamed of their sins. They were sorry that they had turned away from God.

Ezra and Nehemiah reminded the people of God's faithfulness. The people spent half a day remembering God's goodness and praying to him.

"Blessed be your name," the people said. "You alone are God."

Here are some of the things they remembered and what the people prayed to God.

They said, "God, you created the world. You chose Abram and named him Abraham. You promised to give him this land and make him into a great nation. You kept your promise because you, God, are righteous.

"You rescued our ancestors from Egypt. You sent signs and wonders to Pharaoh. You showed your power and might. You divided the sea. You led the people with a cloud by day and a pillar of fire at night.

"You gave the people rules to follow because your commands are good.

"You provided for them with manna and fresh water," they said.

The people remembered God had always provided for them in many ways. They even remembered how the people had rebelled during the time of Moses but that God was forgiving.

The people just kept praising God and remembering!

They remembered how God had taken care of them in Babylon and then returned them to their homeland. The people praised God because he'd never stopped loving them. Never, ever, ever. Even when they'd messed up big, he'd just kept right on loving them.

After this, the people dedicated the walls of Jerusalem with a huge celebration. They rejoiced because God had given them great happiness to be home again. Men, women, and children—everyone rejoiced that day.

In fact, the rejoicing was so loud that it could be heard for miles and miles!

God had brought them home.

Reflection

- Have you ever made a promise that you didn't keep?

- Why was it hard to keep that promise?

- Has anyone ever broken a promise to you?

- How did that make you feel?

- God never breaks a promise! God had kept his promise to his people, just like always.

- God always does what he says he will do. He keeps his promises to us. He wants to be our God forever and ever.

Prayer

Dear God, thank you for your love that lasts always. Thank you that you keep your promises, that you do what you say you'll do. I'm especially glad that one of those promises is you'll love me forever. Amen.

Esther

ESTHER 1–8

After being invaded by enemies, many of God's people were forced to live in the enemies' countries, far away from their own homeland. A young lady named Esther lived with her cousin, Mordecai, in a place called Persia. Mordecai had adopted his young cousin because her parents were no longer alive.

King Xerxes ruled over the empire of Persia. When his wife, Queen Vashti, disobeyed her husband, he chose to kick her out of the palace.

"Get a new queen," his advisors told him.

The king's officials gathered young, unmarried women from all over the empire and brought them to the palace. Beautiful Esther was one of those young women.

"Do not tell them you are a Jewish girl," Mordecai told her.

Sometimes, God's chosen ones were called *Jews* because they were from the country of *Judah*. Mordecai feared the king might not like Esther if he knew she was one of God's chosen people.

For 12 months, servants gave the young women beauty treatments and taught them how to dress like a queen.

That's a long beauty pageant, right? And a lot of bubble baths!

Esther's beauty helped her to stand out. But Esther won the favor of the king's servants and helpers because she was gentle and kind. When it was Esther's turn to visit the king, she won his favor too, with her beauty and kindness.

Which do you think is more important? Good looks or kindness? That's one of those questions we all know the answer to—kindness is much more important than good looks! What's on the inside, in the heart, matters most of all!

The king gave Esther a crown and made her his queen.

All this time, Mordecai stayed near the palace to check on his cousin. One day, a man named Haman arrived.

"Why won't you kneel when I pass by?" Haman asked Mordecai. Haman was second in command at the palace. He expected everyone to kneel before him.

"I am a Jew, and we only pay honor to God," Mordecai answered.

Haman was so full of pride and anger that he wanted to punish Mordecai. He thought, *In fact, I'll get rid of all the Jewish people.*

Haman tricked the king into signing a decree against God's people.

When Mordecai heard what the evil Haman planned to do, he sent a message to Esther. "You can save our people," Mordecai told her. "Esther, you have to tell the king what Haman is planning. Beg for mercy for our people."

Esther reminded Mordecai that it was against the law to approach the king without receiving a request from the king first.

"You must try," Mordecai said. "This could be the very reason you became queen, for such a time as this, to save our people."

Queen Esther feared for her life, but she knew she had to try to save the Jewish families. Esther told Mordecai, "Tell our people to gather and fast and pray for three days. After three days, I will go to the king."

On the third day, Queen Esther dressed in her royal robes and went to see the king.

Thankfully, the king allowed Esther to approach the throne. He said, "Tell me what you want, and you will have it."

At first, Esther didn't tell him about Haman's plans. She invited the king and Haman to a *banquet*, which is a special dinner. And at that banquet, she invited them to another banquet.

Do you think Esther was too scared to tell the king at the first banquet? Have you ever put off saying something you were too scared to say?

Finally, at the second banquet, Esther told the king about Haman's plot. "Haman wants to kill me and all my people."

The king was furious with Haman for his evil plot and his trickery. He sent Haman away. Then the king gave Mordecai an important job position.

The king couldn't take back the royal decree against the Jewish people. Instead, he made another decree. He said, "The Jewish people can fight back and protect themselves."

The Jewish people celebrated with a big feast. Brave Queen Esther had saved her people!

Reflection

- Queen Esther showed great courage when she approached the king uninvited. She knew she might lose her life. That was the rule of kings back then. She probably prayed and asked God for courage. Then she risked her life to save her people.

- What's the hardest thing you've ever done?

- Did you pray and ask God for courage?

- We can ask God for courage to do hard things!

Prayer

Dear God, thank you for people in the Bible, like Esther, who teach me to be brave. Help me remember that I can ask you for courage to do hard things.

Show me what you want me to do for you, God, and give me courage to get the job done. Amen.

PART TWO

New Testament

The Birth of Jesus

LUKE 1:26–38; 2:1–21; MATTHEW 1:18–2:11

Long after God's people had returned home to their own country, a wonderful and exciting thing happened. This amazing thing was part of God's plan to save the whole world from sin and evil. A way to restore people's relationships with God.

Someone was about to arrive—a Savior.

Now, you might think this person arriving would be a fancy king with tons of money and fame and importance. A person who would blast onto the scene with huge celebrations and fireworks.

But that's not what happened.

The greatest story of all began not with a fancy king but with a kind young woman named Mary.

Mary was going about her day, maybe sweeping her kitchen floor, when suddenly an angel appeared to her.

"Greetings," the angel said. "You are highly favored. The Lord is with you."

The angel had just given Mary the biggest surprise of her young life! But he was about to give her an even bigger one.

The angel told her that God wanted her to be the mother of his Son, Jesus.

Mary couldn't believe it! Her people had heard for years that God would send a Savior. Mary's parents had likely taught her God's prophecies about it. But she'd had no idea that *she* would be part of God's biggest plan ever.

Mary was engaged to a carpenter named Joseph. At first, Joseph had a hard time believing the news. But an angel appeared to him too and told him about Jesus. So Joseph took Mary home to be his wife.

Just before the birth of baby Jesus, the leader of the Roman Empire, which now ruled over Israel, ordered everybody in Israel to travel to their hometowns. The Roman leader wanted to count the people and make sure they were paying taxes.

It was a long journey for pregnant Mary to take.

When Mary and Joseph arrived in Joseph's hometown of Bethlehem, lots and lots of people were there to check in and pay taxes. Joseph looked everywhere for a place to spend the night. But there were no rooms anywhere! An innkeeper told Joseph that he had no room for them. So Joseph and Mary went to the place where animals slept.

Say what? If you had a choice, would you rather sleep in a guest room with a nice, soft bed and fluffy pillows or on the ground next to stinky, smelly, noisy animals?

Because all the guest rooms in the town of Bethlehem were filled, Mary and Joseph didn't have a choice. They'd be bunking with the animals.

Soon, baby Jesus entered the world! Mary wrapped her precious baby boy in cloths and laid him in a manger full of hay.

Can you imagine? The holy Son of God slept in the animals' feeding trough!

As soon as Jesus was born, angels appeared to shepherds in a nearby field.

Shepherds? God's holy Son was just born, and angels told shepherds? Yep-a-doodle! You might think the angels would tell important leaders and royal people instead. But God had other plans. He wanted everybody to know about his Son, and he started with the most common people of all—shepherds.

After the angels told the shepherds about the baby, the shepherds hurried to Bethlehem to visit baby Jesus. Once they had seen him, the shepherds told everybody they met!

"Christ is born!" said one shepherd.

"God's Son is here!" said another.

"The Savior of the world is born!" announced a third.

Sometime later, important people called *Magi*, or wise men, who had also learned about the birth of Jesus, traveled a long time to see him. The wise men followed a star that led them to God's Son. When they found Jesus, they presented him with treasures.

God's special Son was here! God's promise had come to life in the form of a baby. And everyone rejoiced and celebrated.

Common shepherds and important wise men celebrated.

Angels and innkeepers celebrated.

Mary and Joseph celebrated.

Most likely, even the animals in the stable knew the baby was special, and they celebrated too.

How do you celebrate the birthday of baby Jesus?

Reflection

- What's the biggest celebration or party you've ever attended?

- How excited were you to be there?

- When God first created the world, he knew that one day he would send a Savior to earth to rescue people from sin. That time was finally here. God sent his only Son, Jesus, into the world. It was a grand day to celebrate!

- God had kept his promise. God's plan was unfolding, and the people of Israel rejoiced!

Prayer

Dear God, thank you for baby Jesus. Thank you for sending your one and only Son to earth to save me from my sins.

Thank you for loving me that much.

Thank you for the reminder that you want everyone to know about Jesus, from the important people to the not-as-important people. Because to you, God, everyone is special and important! I'm so glad that includes me! Amen.

Twelve-Year-Old Jesus in the Temple

LUKE 2:41–52

Every year, Mary and Joseph made the long journey to Jerusalem to celebrate Passover. That was a special festival to remind God's people of the time he'd protected Israel's firstborn sons from the final plague in Egypt.

When Jesus was 12, the family packed up supplies for the trip. They loaded the donkeys and set off on the journey. Lots of family and friends always journeyed to the Passover feast together, in a big group. It took a long time to get to Jerusalem, and the families would stop along the way to spend the night somewhere.

It probably felt like a traveling family reunion, with kids walking and playing with each other along the way, and adults walking and talking together while leading the donkeys.

What's the longest trip you've ever taken? Do you think you'd like to ride a donkey that far? Well, nobody had cars back then, so all of God's people rode donkeys or camels or walked to Jerusalem. That took lots of dedication to make the trip, right?

The Passover festival lasted for a week. Together, the people sang praises to God and worshipped him. God wanted his people to honor and remember him. God wanted his people to worship him often and especially on major occasions, like Passover.

Does your family remember to worship God often and on special days too? What's your favorite special day to worship God? Christmas? Easter? Thanksgiving?

After the Passover festival, Mary and Joseph packed up their things and headed for home with their big group of relatives.

Well, what Mary and Joseph didn't know was that young Jesus had stayed behind in Jerusalem.

I'll bet you're wondering how in the world they didn't even notice that their son was missing! Since friends and family traveled together to get back home, Mary and Joseph thought Jesus was somewhere else in the group, walking with his cousins or friends.

At the end of the first day's travel, Mary and Joseph couldn't find Jesus.

His parents checked with everyone in the group.

"Have you seen Jesus?" Joseph asked everyone.

"Where's my son?" Mary asked.

Worried now, Mary and Joseph rushed back to Jerusalem. They searched for Jesus three days.

Can you imagine being missing that long? That must have been a scary time for Mary and Joseph.

After three long days, Mary and Joseph found Jesus in the temple courts. Twelve-year-old Jesus sat with the older teachers and priests, listening to them and asking questions.

Even though he was a boy, Jesus asked good questions and gave great answers. The teachers were amazed at how much Jesus knew about God!

How does this kid know all this? one teacher might have thought.

Who is this boy? another one might have wondered.

This kid has a gift, another teacher could have thought.

Mary said to Jesus, "Son, why have you frightened us like this? We've looked everywhere for you!"

Young Jesus said, "Didn't you know that I had to be in my Father's house?"

Mary and Joseph believed that Jesus was God's Son. But they didn't understand everything that would happen when Jesus grew up. They were just happy to have found their son again!

Jesus knew he would do God's special work when he got older. But he also knew that obeying his earthly parents was part of God's will for him.

The Bible says that "Jesus grew in wisdom and stature and in favor with God and man." That means Jesus was wise and grew tall and that God and people liked him.

Jesus was a good son to Mary and Joseph. He obeyed his parents and treated others with kindness. He worshipped and obeyed God.

The Savior of the world was God's perfect and holy Son.

Reflection

- What's your favorite Bible story?

- Why do you like that one best?

- God loves for his children to learn more about him. God wants to have a relationship with his children. We can do that when we study his words in the Bible and talk to him often in prayer.

- God also wants his children to be obedient to him, like young Jesus was. And obeying parents is an important way to obey God too!

Prayer

Dear God, thank you for Bible stories about Jesus that teach me how to live the way you want me to live. Help me want to know more and more about you.

Lead me to listen to my parents and teachers so I can learn everything you want me to learn. Amen.

John Baptizes Jesus

LUKE 1:5–25; 1:57–66; 3:1–23; MARK 1:1–11

Just before Jesus was born, Mary's cousin, Elizabeth, gave birth to a baby boy. Elizabeth and her husband, Zechariah, knew their son would become a special man of God.

How did they know that? Because an angel had appeared to them and told them!

Here's what happened.

Zechariah and Elizabeth were older and had no kids. An angel appeared to Zechariah at the temple.

"Don't be afraid," the angel said.

That's the first thing most angels said back then. Why? Because the sudden appearance of an angel usually startled people. Would you be a little scared too? Or would you enjoy meeting an angel?

The angel told Zechariah that his wife would have a baby. "Call him John," the angel said. "He'll bring the people of Israel back to God. And he'll prepare the way for God's Son."

"How can my wife and I have a baby at our age?" Zechariah asked.

Perhaps Zechariah shouldn't have asked such a silly question. God can do anything! Why would Zechariah even question the angel?

ZAP! Zechariah could no longer talk.

The angel said, "My name is Gabriel, and I stand in the presence of God. Because you did not believe my words, you will not speak until the baby is born."

Don't you think Zechariah wished he'd never doubted God? Is it sometimes hard for you to believe God's words in the Bible? God can be trusted to do everything he says he'll do. God is faithful.

Well, just like the angel said, Elizabeth delivered a baby boy sometime later.

Zechariah wrote on a piece of paper, "His name is John." And, POOF! Zechariah could speak again!

I'm thinking Zechariah had learned his lesson. He probably didn't doubt God again!

John grew to be a man of God, but he didn't live like other Israelites. He made his clothes from camel hair and lived in the wilderness.

And guess what he ate? Locusts and honey. Ick! If you had to eat bugs for dinner, would you rather eat a crunchy grasshopper or a fuzzy bumblebee?

People from all over traveled to see John. He told people about God. He told them to repent, to turn away from their sins.

Many people listened to him. They wanted to follow God. They promised to worship only the Lord and serve him.

John baptized a lot of people in the Jordan River. He explained to the people that going under the water and coming up again was a symbol of washing away their sins. Getting clean from the bad things in their lives.

Some people asked John if he was the one God had promised to send to save the world.

"I'm not the one," John said. "I come to prepare the way for God's Son."

John told the people how God wanted them to live.

"Share your clothes with people who don't have enough clothes to wear," he said. "Share your food with people who don't have enough to eat."

John told the tax collectors to stop cheating people. He said, "Don't take more money than you are supposed to take."

He also told people the good news about the Savior. "One more powerful than me will come. He will baptize you with the Holy Spirit."

One day, John stood waist-deep in the river. He proclaimed the good news and told people to stop sinning. John baptized the people who said they wanted to worship God and turn from their sins.

Jesus arrived and asked John to baptize him too. Jesus was perfect. Jesus didn't have sins to wash away. But he wanted to show the other people what to do. It was part of God's plan.

So John baptized Jesus.

When Jesus came up from the water, the heavens opened, and a dove flew to Jesus. Only, it wasn't just a dove. It was the Spirit of God. The Holy Spirit landed on Jesus, and God's voice from heaven said, "This is my Son, whom I love. I am very pleased with him."

After Jesus had been baptized, it was time for him to start his ministry!

Reflection

- John was part of God's plan to prepare people's hearts for Jesus.

- We can be part of God's plan to tell other people about Jesus too. We can use our words and our actions to prepare others' hearts for Jesus. We can show people how to live by loving God and worshipping him and being kind to everyone.

- Who can you tell about Jesus tomorrow?

- What will you say to that person?

Prayer

Dear God, thank you that Jesus came to save the world. Help me be kind to everyone so that others see my kindness and learn what Jesus is like.

Help me to use kind words and actions to prepare the hearts of others for Jesus.

I love you, God. Amen.

Friends Bring a
Paralyzed Man to Jesus

MARK 2:1–12

God sent his perfect, holy Son, Jesus, to the world to save Israel . . . and to save people from all other nations. The world had become a sinful place. Everyone needed a Savior to take away their sins. People also needed to learn more about their wonderful God.

Jesus went all over Israel teaching about God. He taught in the temple. He taught in the courts. He taught in the streets. He taught in the fields. He taught from a boat. He taught in the wilderness.

He traveled all over just to tell as many people as he could about God. Jesus wanted to heal their hearts. He wanted them to turn their lives back to God. And he wanted them to have a relationship with God, like a child has with a kind and loving parent.

Jesus had compassion on the people. He loved all of God's children because Jesus was also God.

He once said the people were like lost sheep without a shepherd. Jesus wanted to be their shepherd. He wanted to guide them and take care of them.

As Jesus traveled and taught, he saw that people had many needs. Some people were sick. Some couldn't use their legs to walk. Some couldn't talk. Many couldn't see. Others couldn't hear. A lot of people didn't have enough money to buy food or clothes. Some widows had no one to take care of them. Some children didn't have parents to live with.

Jesus cared about everyone's needs. So, all over Israel, Jesus taught and healed people.

Word spread quickly about the amazing Son of God. People came from everywhere to hear him speak and to be healed. In fact, most of them wanted their physical bodies healed more than they wanted their hearts healed.

One day, Jesus went to speak in a town called Capernaum.

"Jesus is coming," one man whispered to another.

"Jesus is coming," the next person said a little louder.

"Let's go see Jesus," a woman told her friend.

"I'm going to meet Jesus!" a child yelled excitedly.

Pretty soon, the house where Jesus was staying began to spill over with people eager to see and hear him.

Elbows and arms and legs and feet and sandals were everywhere. The people squished in tighter to make room for more. EVERYONE wanted to see and hear Jesus.

Four friends who'd heard about Jesus wanted to bring their friend to Jesus to be healed. Their friend was *paralyzed*, which means he couldn't walk. The four friends carried him on a mat to the house in Capernaum.

So many people were there that the friends couldn't get in.

"I've got an idea," one of them said. (If this had been a cartoon, a lightbulb would've appeared above the man's head!) He said, "Let's uncover part of the roof and lower our friend down that way."

The friends climbed up on the roof, making sure not to drop their friend.

This is one of those "don't try this at home" kinds of stories, right?

The friends pulled back part of the roof and lowered their paralyzed friend inside, right in front of Jesus.

Jesus was impressed with the men's faith. He knew if they had gone to that much trouble to bring the paralyzed man to see him, then they believed he was the Son of God.

"Your sins are forgiven," he told the paralyzed man.

Some of the teachers of the law who sat there were shocked at Jesus' words. Their jaws fell open. They whispered among themselves, "Just who does this Jesus think he is? Only God can forgive sins!"

The teachers didn't understand that Jesus is God. He is God in human form.

Jesus wanted to prove that he had the power to forgive sins. So Jesus told the paralyzed man, "Stand up and walk."

The paralyzed man stood up and walked home.

Jesus had shown everyone there that he is God. He had shown that he can heal people *and* forgive our sins.

Reflection

- When have you helped a friend?

- These four friends loved their paralyzed friend so much that they wanted him to see Jesus. They knew Jesus could heal him.

- Like them, you can be a good friend by taking care of someone's needs. But it's even more important to take care of their spiritual needs, to take care of their heart. In other words, it's important to tell them about Jesus, their Savior!

Prayer

Dear God, show me how to be a wonderful friend to others. Help me be willing to take care of their needs.

If I know someone is sad, help me offer kindness. If I know someone is hungry, help me offer them food. If I know someone needs money, help me share what I have.

Help me take care of people's needs. But even more importantly, help me always tell others about Jesus. Amen.

Jesus Heals Many People

MATTHEW 8:5–13; MARK 5:21–43

Jesus walked around much of the country, preaching and teaching and healing and talking. He met lots of people with lots of needs. He knew that many people were hurting. Jesus offered kindness and compassion everywhere he went.

"God loves you forever and ever," Jesus said.

"God wants you to know him and love him," Jesus said.

"God wants you to know and love me, God's Son," he said. "I will love you forever too."

Jesus offered love and hope. Never before had anyone offered love and hope like Jesus did.

God sent Jesus to his chosen people, the Israelites, first. God planned to show Jesus to the entire world through his chosen people.

Many people believed in Jesus. Even people from neighboring countries. Even Roman soldiers who ruled Israel.

One Roman soldier believed Jesus was God's Son. When the Roman soldier's servant became ill, the soldier knew just what to do. He hurried to find Jesus.

"Jesus, my servant is paralyzed and in great pain," the soldier said.

"I'll come and heal him," Jesus said.

The Roman solider didn't feel worthy to have Jesus inside his home. He knew he wasn't part of God's chosen people. But his faith was strong. He believed Jesus could heal his servant even if Jesus were far away from the servant.

"Lord, I am not worthy that you should come into my house," the soldier said. "Please just say the word, and I know my servant will be healed."

The soldier's faith impressed Jesus. Jesus knew that many of the Israelites' hearts were hard, and they didn't have the faith of this Roman soldier.

"Go on your way," Jesus said. "This very moment, your servant is healed."

How do you think the Roman soldier felt right then? Do you think he ran all the way home to check on his servant? Who do you think he told about his servant's miraculous healing? Most likely, the Roman soldier told everybody he met about the miraculous way Jesus had healed his servant.

On another day, Jesus healed a man's daughter. Actually, Jesus brought her back to life.

Here is what happened.

A man named Jairus worked in a *synagogue*. That's another name for God's house of worship. Jairus, the synagogue leader, hurried to find Jesus because his little daughter was very sick. Jairus loved his daughter dearly, and he knew Jesus could heal her.

"My daughter is dying," Jairus said when he found Jesus.

Jesus had compassion on the man. Jesus started walking after Jairus to his home.

As always, large crowds followed Jesus, looking for healing from their diseases. Jesus healed a woman as they walked.

Before the two men could get to Jairus' home, someone found Jairus and said, "Your daughter is no longer living."

Jesus told Jairus, "Don't be afraid. Keep believing."

When they got to Jairus' house, Jesus went to the little girl's room, along with her mother and father. Jesus took her hand and said, "Little girl, I say to you, stand up."

And I bet you can guess what happened, right? The little girl stood up from the bed, alive again.

Everyone in the house was stunned and thankful!

Wherever Jesus went, he amazed the people with his healing miracles.

But remember, Jesus was more concerned about people's hearts and faith. He wanted them to know God and follow God. But he also cared about their needs.

Jesus showed he was the Son of God by performing miracles and healing those who were sick or hurt. He told people that if they trusted in him and believed he was the Son of God, their hearts could be healed too.

Then they could one day live in heaven with God forever.

Reflection

- When you don't feel well, do you pray and ask Jesus to help you feel better?

- Jesus showed his power each time he healed someone. No one had ever performed the kind of miracles that Jesus did.

- Many people had faith that Jesus would heal them. When we are sick or injured, God wants us to have that kind of faith too. We can ask God to help us believe that he will heal us.

Prayer

Dear God, please bless me with strong faith. The Bible tells me that you can do anything, and I want to always believe that.

Sometimes, my faith wobbles when times get tough. When that happens, help me to trust you and ask you for more faith.

Grow my faith stronger and stronger every day! Amen.

Jesus Feeds 5000

LUKE 5:1-11; MARK 1:16-20; 2:13-14;
3:13-19; MATTHEW 14:13-21

Jesus asked a group of men to stay with him and help him teach people about God.

Here is how he chose them.

One day, Jesus climbed into a boat that belonged to a man named Simon Peter. Jesus said, "Take me out to the deep water."

Simon Peter and his brother, Andrew, were fishermen. They did as Jesus asked.

Then Jesus told them, "Lower your fishing nets into the water."

Simon Peter said, "Master, we've fished all night and haven't caught anything."

But, because they knew about Jesus, they did just what he said.

You won't believe what happened next! Well, you probably will, because, after all, it's Jesus we're talking about.

The net filled with so many fish that the boat almost sank!

"Help!" Simon Peter and Andrew yelled for their friends, James and John, to bring their boat and help. It took all four men to pull the net to shore filled with the ginormous load of fish.

Jesus told them, "Follow me, and I will make you fishers of men."

The men put down their nets immediately and followed Jesus.

Later, Jesus asked Matthew to be his disciple. Matthew was a tax collector. Many people didn't trust tax collectors because they often took more money than they should.

Sometimes, Jesus picked unlikely people to be his helpers.

Jesus had many helpers and followers, but these 12 became his special ones, called apostles: Simon Peter, Andrew, James, John, Matthew (also called Levi), Philip, Bartholomew (also called Nathanael), Thomas, James (the son of Alphaeus), Thaddaeus (also called Jude), Simon the Zealot, and Judas Iscariot.

Jesus taught them to teach people about God. He even gave them the power to heal people who were sick or hurt.

One day, Jesus and his disciples took a boat across a lake. They wanted to get away from the large crowd of people for a short rest. But guess what happened?

Word traveled fast.

More than 5000 people walked from nearby towns to come see Jesus.

Jesus felt compassion for the people. He healed and talked and healed and preached and healed and hugged. Jesus loved the people, and the people loved him. The crowd listened to every word Jesus said.

The sun began to set, but no one had even thought about dinner!

One disciple said, "Jesus, how will we feed all these people?"

And another one said, "We don't have enough money to feed this many people."

And one more disciple said, "We've collected five loaves of bread and two fish. That's all the food we could find."

Jesus told the people to sit in the grass. Jesus looked to heaven and prayed a blessing over the food. He tore the bread into pieces and broke off pieces of fish.

Then the disciples handed out the food.

Jesus pulled the bread into pieces.

The disciples shared it with the people.

Jesus divided the fish into pieces.

The disciples shared it with the people.

Until every single person had food to eat for dinner.

When the crowd of people had finished eating, the 12 disciples collected all the leftovers in baskets.

How many baskets of leftovers do you think they collected?

Twelve!

Why do you think that was the exact number of baskets of food? Do you think Jesus was trying to teach the disciples something special, as well as all the people in the crowd?

Jesus taught the people that God provides for every one of them.

He told them—and showed them—how much God loved them.

Reflection

- What helps you to feel God's love?

- Jesus used miracles to show God's power and love. Jesus wanted the people to know that there was no one as mighty and powerful as God. He also wanted them to know that God was the only true God. No fake god and no other person could love them and care for them like God did.

- The people believed in the signs and wonders of Jesus.

Prayer

Dear God, you are mighty and powerful. No one can do the things you do. Thank you that you love me enough to take care of my physical needs, like providing good food to eat.

And thank you for sending your Son, Jesus, to make my heart feel happy and blessed. Amen.

The Good Samaritan

LUKE 10:25-37

Jesus taught the Israelites using the scrolls and Scriptures written by people from long ago, writers like Moses, David, Solomon, and the prophets. Jesus wanted the Israelites to know what God's Word said.

One day when Jesus was teaching the people about God, a man who had studied God's Scriptures tried to trick Jesus. Many people believed Jesus was God's Son and followed him. But some people doubted Jesus. They tried to trick him with their words.

"Teacher," the expert of the law said. "What must I do to inherit eternal life?"

Jesus knew the man wanted to trick him. So he asked, "What is written in God's laws?"

The man answered, "Love the Lord your God with all your heart, and with all your soul, and with all your strength, and with all your mind. And love your neighbor as yourself."

"You have answered correctly," Jesus said. "Do this and you will inherit eternal life."

Then the man asked another question. "Who is my neighbor?"

Jesus told a story to help him understand. Jesus said, "A man traveled alone from Jerusalem to Jericho. Robbers attacked the traveler. The robbers hit the man and hurt him. Then they left him alone on the side of the road and ran away with the man's belongings.

"After a while, a priest came down the same road. When he saw the hurt man, he walked all the way around him on the other side of the road. The priest did not help the injured man.

"Next, a man from the family of Levi passed by. He too crossed on the other side of the road, away from the hurt man. He didn't help the injured guy, either.

"The third man to come along the road was from Samaria."

Now, dear readers, most Samaritans and Jewish people lived near each other, but they did not get along. Can you guess what the Samaritan did when he saw the injured Jewish man? Do you think he went to the other side of the road, like the priest and the Levite had done? Listen to the rest of the story.

Jesus said, "The Samaritan man felt sorry for the injured Jewish man. He cleaned the man's wounds, put medicine on them, and wrapped the wounds with bandages. Then he put the man on his own donkey and brought him to the nearest town. He stayed with him all night and took care of him.

"The next day, the Samaritan paid the innkeeper so that the hurt man could stay another night. He told the innkeeper to take care of the man. And he offered to pay more money, if it was needed, when he came back to the inn."

When Jesus finished talking, he asked the expert of the law, "Who do you think was a neighbor to the hurt man?"

Readers, do you know the answer? Of course you do! It was the Samaritan, right?

Jesus wanted the expert of the law to understand that a neighbor can be anybody, not just the person who lives next door to you.

A neighbor can be someone you know really, really well or a stranger you see at the grocery store.

A neighbor can be a friend or an enemy.

A neighbor can be a poor person or a rich person.

A neighbor can have dark skin or light skin.

A neighbor can have clean, fancy clothes or torn, dirty clothes.

A neighbor can have a huge house or no house at all.

A neighbor can be a wise man or a shepherd in a field.

Jesus wanted the expert of the law to know—just like he wants us to know—that God loves every single person on earth. And he wants us to treat every person with kindness.

Reflection

- Is there someone in your neighborhood, or class, or church who is difficult for you to love?

- God loves that person just as much as he loves you!

- God wants us to love Jesus with our whole heart. And God wants us to love each other, no matter who a person is, or what they look like, or where they come from, or who they know. God says we are to love everybody.

Prayer

Dear God, help me remember to love you with all my heart, and all my soul, and all my strength, and all my mind.

And help me to love my neighbor, God. Help me love and care about all people, not just people who look and act like me. Show me how to love like the Good Samaritan did. Amen.

Mary, Martha, and Lazarus

LUKE 10:38–42; JOHN 11:1–44

Jesus walked from place to place, telling people about God and healing them. Many people invited him to stay in their homes. When Jesus visited the town of Bethany, he stayed with his friends Mary, Martha, and Lazarus. The two sisters and one brother lived together and took care of one another.

Whenever Jesus stopped by, Martha busied herself cooking and cleaning and taking care of him. She often stayed so busy that she didn't even take time to visit with Jesus.

Martha's sister, Mary, sat at Jesus' feet and listened to his every word. She didn't want to miss anything Jesus said!

Martha sprinkled the flour.

Martha poured the oil.

Martha mixed the dough.

Martha rolled the bread.

Martha baked the bread.

Martha swept the floor.

Martha wiped the table.

Martha washed the dishes.

Martha never stopped working to listen to Jesus. She didn't take time to be with the Savior of the world.

Do you get busy doing a bunch of things and forget to spend time with Jesus? Do you clean your room and fold the clothes and do your homework and watch TV and talk to your friends and go to softball practice and play at the park and take care of your brother or sister and . . . never make time for Jesus?

Martha complained to Jesus. She said, "Jesus, I am doing all the work. My sister isn't helping me with anything. Please tell her to help me work."

Jesus said to her, "Martha, you are worried about too many things. Mary has chosen what is most important. Mary is spending time with me."

Jesus knew Martha's chores were important. He knew those things had to get done sometime. But he also knew that the most important thing at that moment was to spend time with God.

Homework and chores are super important. Those things have to get done. Even cleaning your room—ugh—is important and has to get done.

God knows all those things are important. But none of those things is more important than God. We need to be responsible, but we also need to make time every day for Jesus.

How do you think Martha felt when Jesus answered her? Do you think she stopped her chores and came to sit with Jesus too? Hopefully, that's what she did. Because that was most important.

Sometime later, Jesus learned that Lazarus was very sick. Jesus loved Mary, Martha, and Lazarus very much. They were his dear friends. Hearing that Lazarus was sick made Jesus sad.

Before Jesus could get to Bethany, Lazarus died. That made Jesus even sadder. The Bible says that Jesus cried when he heard the news.

By the time Jesus got to the tomb where Lazarus was buried, Lazarus had been dead for four days. Even so, Jesus asked for the stone covering the tomb to be rolled away.

Jesus prayed out loud, "Father, thank you for hearing my prayer. You always hear my prayer, but I say this so the people here will believe you sent me." Then Jesus called for Lazarus. "Lazarus, come out."

With the grave cloths still wrapped around him, Lazarus walked out of the tomb, looking sort of like a wobbly mummy. But Lazarus was alive! Jesus had raised him from the dead.

The people could hardly believe what they were seeing!

Now the people knew that Jesus could do anything.

Reflection

- Do you make time for Jesus every day? Do you read the Bible and talk to God in prayer?

- God loves us so much that he wants us to spend time with him.

- Just think about it—if you never spent time with your friends, your parents, your grandparents, or your pet, do you think you'd feel very close to them? Spending time with God helps us feel close to him.

Prayer

Dear God, help me be like Mary and remember what is most important. Help me make time for you every day.

I want to feel close to you, and spending time with you is the best way to do that. Thank you for loving me so much that you want to spend time with me too. Amen.

Jesus and the Children

MATTHEW 19:13–15;
MARK 10:13–16; LUKE 18:15–17

For three years, Jesus taught people about God. He said and did so many things that even a houseful of books couldn't hold all the stories!

Jesus told thousands and thousands of people about God. Jesus wanted everybody to know how much God loved them. He wanted them to turn from their sins and choose to do good and kind things.

He told everyone, "If you want to live in heaven forever with God, you need to believe that God sent me, his Son, to save the world. Believe in me, and you can have eternal life." Jesus taught the people that God offered forgiveness of sins. He told everyone to forgive others too, just like God forgave them.

He said that the 10 Commandments could be summed up in just two: love God and love other people. When we do those two, Jesus said, we are actually obeying all 10.

Everywhere he went during those three years—and he walked to a LOT of places—Jesus talked about God.

Jesus also did all sorts of miracles. He healed people who were sick or had diseases. He healed those with mental illnesses. He raised people from the dead.

Jesus gave rest to those who were weary and tired. He comforted the sad and lonely. He fed the hungry.

And he told the people that he had springs of *living water*. "Come to me, and you'll never be thirsty again," he said.

Living water? Are you wondering what Jesus meant by that? He wasn't saying that after a hot day at the beach or in the backyard you wouldn't want a drink of water. Jesus meant that trusting in him refreshes the soul and gives contentment.

Jesus did many, many important things.

One day, Jesus did something that no one thought was important. At least, not at first.

On this particular day, parents brought their children to Jesus. They wanted Jesus to bless their little ones. They wanted their kids to see and know Jesus.

The disciples might have thought Jesus was too tired to take time for the children. Or maybe they thought Jesus had more important work to do that day. For some reason, the disciples scolded the parents for bothering Jesus.

But Jesus said, "Let the little children come to me!"

Can you imagine Jesus throwing his arms wide open and letting the little kids run to him? Don't you think he probably scooped up some of the littlest ones? Can you just imagine him giving bear hugs to the big kids? Do you think he tried to see how many he could fit on his lap at one time?

Have you ever climbed onto your mom's or dad's lap with your siblings or cousins or friends? How many kids piled onto your mom's or dad's lap that day?

When Jesus spent time with those children, what do you think Jesus and the kids talked about?

Can't you just imagine some of the conversations?

"Jesus, I lost a tooth today!"

"Jesus, I stubbed my toe yesterday."

"Jesus, my grandma is sick."

"Jesus, we're moving next week."

"Jesus, I need help with math."

"Jesus, I need a friend."

"Jesus, I got a new bike!"

Well, maybe they didn't talk about bikes.

Jesus wanted his disciples—and all the adults—to know how much he loved little children.

Jesus loves children. All the children of the world. Wait—there's a song about that!

But it's true. Jesus loves every child. Every hair color and eye color and skin color. From the richest to the poorest, from the tallest to the shortest. Jesus loves them all.

Jesus reminded his disciples that even adults should have childlike faith. He wanted them to know that every adult needed a trusting heart, just like a child's, to believe in Jesus.

All God's children, of all ages, are precious to our Savior!

Reflection

- How do your parents and teachers show their love to you?

- In what ways do you show love to them?

- What helps you feel the love of Jesus?

- Jesus also wanted people to know that he loves and cares about them and that he especially loves and cares about children. He loves children, and he wants them to love him too.

- What can you do tomorrow to show Jesus that you love him?

Prayer

Dear God, thank you that Jesus showed us how much you love children. I'm so glad Jesus loves me!

Thank you that I can talk to Jesus whenever I want. Thank you for the promise that Jesus hears my every prayer.

Thank you, Jesus, for coming to this world to save everybody—big people and little children too. Amen.

Zaccheus Meets Jesus

LUKE 19:1–10

When Jesus entered the town of Jericho, word spread quickly of his arrival.

"Jesus is here," one man might have said to another.

"It's Jesus—the one everybody's talking about," that man may have told another.

"God's Son is passing through," a woman could have told her friend.

"He's the one who heals the sick and raises the dead," some may have said excitedly.

"Mary and Joseph's son," the town carpenter might have said.

"He's come to save the world," one of the children could have mentioned.

"Jesus is a very smart man," another man may have said.

"He knows all about God," the man's wife could have answered.

"Jesus loves me," one of the children may have exclaimed.

In no time, a crowd of people had gathered around Jesus. They wanted to hear everything he had to say. The people asked questions. They listened to his answers. All of Jesus' followers wanted to be near him and learn more about God.

But one person couldn't get near Jesus, no matter how hard he tried. Zacchaeus, a wealthy tax collector, had heard about Jesus, but he'd never seen him before. He was curious about this person so many others were talking about.

Do you know why Zacchaeus couldn't get close to Jesus? Zacchaeus was too short to see over the crowd and too small to push his way to the front of all the people.

Now, Zacchaeus didn't want to miss his chance to see Jesus. And he had an idea. Just down the road, Zacchaeus could see a tall sycamore tree. Its low branches reached close to the ground where he could climb them.

He may not have been a very tall person, but he could certainly run. Zacchaeus ran ahead of the whole crowd of people and went straight to that tree. He grabbed the first branch and pulled himself up, digging the toes of his sandals into the tree trunk. He pulled and pulled and climbed, until he got high enough in the tree that he could see above the heads of everybody on the road.

You might not realize it, but this very small man had some very tall sins in his life.

Many of the tax collectors back in those days took more money from the people than they were supposed to collect.

"You owe the Roman government 20 coins," Zacchaeus might have said to the father of a family, when the family really owed just 12 coins to the Roman government. Then Zacchaeus would keep the extra coins for himself.

Perhaps some of the tax collectors were honest. Sadly, many of them were dishonest. That made the Israelites dislike tax collectors.

Zacchaeus was a chief tax collector. That probably meant he'd taken a LOT more money from the people than he should have, and the Roman government had rewarded him by making him the chief tax collector.

When the crowd of people came close to the tree, Jesus stopped walking and looked up, right at Zacchaeus. Jesus said, "Zacchaeus, come down. I'm staying at your house today."

Zacchaeus was stunned.

The people were shocked.

Zacchaeus probably stumbled over his words. "Okay, Jesus."

The people definitely muttered their words. "Why is Jesus going to a sinner's house?"

Right then, Zacchaeus recognized his sins. He was sorry he'd cheated so many people. He knew cheating was wrong. He knew those sins had hurt God.

He told Jesus he wanted to give half of all he had to the poor. "And anyone I've cheated," Zacchaeus said. "I'll pay back four times the amount."

Zacchaeus' heart changed the minute he met Jesus. He no longer wanted to do wrong things and cheat and harm others. Zacchaeus wanted to do good things. He wanted to help others.

Jesus reminded the crowd of people, who were probably still grumbling, that God had sent Jesus to earth to find the lost sinners and turn them back to God.

And that's no *tall* tale!

Reflection

- Did you do something wrong today?

- Did you ask God to forgive you?

- No matter how short or tall our sins are, God wants us to ask him for forgiveness.

- He also wants us to turn away from our sins. Because God loves us so much, he sent his Son, Jesus, to help us turn away from our sins and turn to God instead. And we can thank him because God loves to forgive.

Prayer

Dear God, please forgive me when I mess up. Forgive me when I am unkind. Forgive me when I say bad words. Forgive me when I talk back to my parents. Forgive me for all the bad things I do. Help me not to ever cheat.

Thank you, God, for your promise of forgiveness.

Lead me to do what is right and good. Thank you for always loving me, God, no matter what. Amen.

The Last Supper

MATTHEW 26:17–28; MARK 14:12–25;
LUKE 22:7–20; JOHN 13:1–17; 14:6

Remember when God rescued his people from Egypt? Remember the final plague that convinced Pharaoh to let God's people go? That night, all the firstborn Egyptian sons died.

Hours before that happened, Moses told each Israelite family to sacrifice a lamb. He told them to paint some of the lamb's blood on the doorposts of their homes. That was a sign for the angel of death to *pass over* those homes and harm no one inside. The Israelites were saved by the blood of the lamb.

Every year after that, God wanted his people to celebrate Passover. This celebration reminded the people of God's rescue a long time ago. And it pointed to a new rescue that would happen one day.

Now, the time had come for God to show his people and the world his ultimate rescue plan. The Lamb of God—Jesus—was God's plan to save everybody from their sins.

Jesus knew it would be his last Passover celebration on earth because he would soon be going back to heaven to live with God.

So he sent two of his disciples to begin preparations for the Passover meal. A kind family let the disciples use their upstairs room.

When Jesus and the other disciples arrived for the Passover supper, some of the disciples may have wondered who might wash their dusty, filthy feet. In those days, because everyone wore sandals and walked on dirt roads, the lowest servant in the household had the disgusting job of washing stinky, sweaty, dirty feet.

Would you want that job? Would you rather wash someone's dirty feet or clean up after your favorite pet? Well, back in those days, because animals trudged along on the same roads as people, washing someone's feet might be a lot like cleaning up after a pet!

Nobody wanted the job.

That evening, there were no foot-washing servants in the home. Can you guess who washed the disciples' feet?

Jesus grabbed a towel and a bowl of water and began washing Peter's feet.

Peter was embarrassed that his Master and Lord was doing such a lowly job.

Jesus told Peter, "You might not understand right now. But if you won't let me wash your feet, you can't be my disciple."

Now Peter did want Jesus to wash his feet!

Jesus washed the feet of every disciple. By doing that, he showed he wanted to serve them and take care of them . . . and that Jesus' followers were to do the same—serve and take care of everybody.

Everyone was clean now, so they felt better. Just like Jesus had done, they could serve and care for other people too, and then the people they helped would also feel better.

During the Passover feast, Jesus took the bread in his hands, gave thanks, and broke it into pieces to give to the disciples. "This is my body," Jesus explained. "My body will be broken in order to save you."

Then Jesus held up his cup of wine and gave thanks. He said, "This is my blood that will take away your sins."

Though the disciples didn't completely understand right then, they would understand later. Jesus was trying to tell the disciples that he was the new covenant. Jesus was God's way to save people from sin. And, in a very sad way, it would cost Jesus his body and his blood—his life—to save the people.

Jesus said to his disciples, "I am the way and the truth and the life. No one can come to God except through me."

Jesus helped them see that he is the bridge between mankind and God. The only way to get to God is through Jesus, by believing in Jesus as the Savior.

After the Passover meal—the last supper he would eat with his disciples—Jesus went to a nearby garden to pray. Jesus knew all about God's plan to save everyone from sin. He also knew that he only had a few hours left on earth. His life would have to end on earth in order to save the world.

Jesus loved everybody so much that he wanted to give his own life to save the world. It was time for God's rescue plan to begin.

Jesus waited in the garden and prayed.

Reflection

- God had a plan from the very beginning of creation to save the world from sin and bring people back to God.

- What can you do tomorrow to show God how thankful you are for Jesus?

- Jesus is the bridge between mankind and God. Accepting Jesus as Savior and Lord is the way to have a relationship with God on earth now and later with him in heaven.

Prayer

Dear God, thank you for sending Jesus to be Savior of the world. Thank you, Jesus, for coming as the Lamb of God to rescue me from my sins.

Help me love others so much that I want to tell them about you. Help me serve others just like you did. Amen.

The Crucifixion and Resurrection

MATTHEW 26:14−16, 47−48;
MARK 14:43−16:8, 19; LUKE 22:1−6;
22:47−24:12, 50−52; JOHN 18−20:18

When Jesus finished praying, a crowd burst into the garden. In the crowd were guards, soldiers, and others sent by the chief priests. Judas, the apostle, led the way. Filled with greed, Judas had secretly made a deal with the chief priests to tell them how to find Jesus. The chief priests had paid Judas 30 pieces of silver.

The chief priests were jealous of Jesus. They didn't believe he was the Son of God. They had tricked the Roman soldiers into believing that Jesus had said he wanted to be king of the land. So the soldiers had come to arrest Jesus.

God's plan wasn't for Jesus to be the king of a country. God's plan was way bigger than that!

But the Roman guards didn't get it.

The chief priests didn't get it.

Judas didn't get it.

Even the apostles and followers didn't understand it completely.

The whole world would soon see, though.

The story gets pretty sad at this point. It's like when you're watching a movie and all those bad things start happening. And the good guy has been captured, and you think the bad guy is going to win.

But God always wins!

Because God is holy and perfect, he cannot tolerate sin. Sin cannot go unpunished. Jesus willingly took on the sins of the world that day, to take away our punishment. This was God's longtime plan to take away the sins of the world.

The guards arrested Jesus and took him to the Roman governor, named Pontius Pilate. Pilate told the chief priests that he could find no wrong in the man they called Jesus. Pilate wanted to let Jesus go free.

But the priests stirred up the crowd, and they yelled, "Crucify him!"

Some of the guards whipped and kicked and hit Jesus. They put a crown of thorns on his head. They dressed him in a purple robe, because purple meant royalty, and they made fun of him.

They spit on him and said, "Hail, king of the Jews." They had no idea that they spoke the truth. They meant for their words to be mean.

The story gets even harder to hear, but I promise it has a really great ending.

The guards forced Jesus to carry a heavy wooden cross up the hill of Golgotha. On top of the hill, guards hammered thick nails through Jesus' hands and feet and into the wooden cross. Then the guards stood up the cross with Jesus on it.

Even though Jesus had lived a perfect, sinless life, he took on every past, present, and future sin of every human being. He loved everyone so much that he was willing to die for them.

He even loved the ones who were punishing him. Jesus said, "Father, forgive them, because they do not understand what they are doing."

Hours later, Jesus said, "It is finished," and took his last breath.

At that very moment, the earth shook violently. Jesus was dead.

A disciple of Jesus took his body to a tomb and placed him there. The disciple rolled a big stone in front of the opening.

Jesus' friends and followers mourned his death.

They had no idea what was about to happen!

Three days later, a follower of Jesus named Mary Magdalene, along with some other women, went to his tomb. The stone had been rolled away. The tomb was empty. And an angel was there!

The angel said, "Jesus is not here. He is risen!"

The women hurried from the tomb. They didn't know whether to be scared or joyful, or a mixture of both!

Suddenly, the women saw Jesus. They bowed and hugged his feet and worshipped him. And they probably cried tears of joy too.

"Do not be afraid," Jesus said. "Go and tell my disciples that I am alive."

Jesus appeared to his disciples several times after he had died and risen again. Now the disciples finally understood God's plan.

Jesus told them he would soon rise up to heaven. But he promised that they too would one day come and live in heaven.

Jesus blessed the disciples. Then, as they stood around him, Jesus floated upward toward the sky. He rose up into heaven.

It's a happy ending—or a new beginning—of God's perfect plan.

Reflection

- When Jesus was crucified, he took the punishment that everyone else deserved. He loves us that much!

- How can you thank God tonight for Jesus?

- When we believe that Jesus is God's Son and that he died on the cross to save us from our sins, salvation is our gift. Salvation allows us to one day live in heaven with God.

- The crucifixion and resurrection had been part of God's perfect plan all along.

Prayer

Dear God, it hurts to know how much Jesus suffered for me and for the world. Help me remember that it was my sins too that put Jesus on the cross.

Thank you, Jesus, for forgiveness and the gift of salvation, so that one day I can live in heaven with you. Amen.

God Sends the Holy Spirit Helper

ACTS 1:1–11; 2

After Jesus came back to life and left the tomb, he appeared to his disciples. Their hearts filled with joy! They were so happy to be in the presence of Jesus again.

Jesus wanted to tell them one more time how much he loved them. And he wanted the disciples to tell everybody in the whole world how much Jesus loved them too.

He said, "Tell people in every nation that they can have forgiveness and salvation if they believe in me."

Just before he went back to heaven, Jesus told the disciples to stay in Jerusalem and wait there for a special gift from God—his wonderful Holy Spirit. Jesus said, "Now that I am going back to live with my Father in heaven, God will send his Holy Spirit to be with you and help you as you teach people about God."

Jesus went back to heaven before their very eyes, rising up into the sky, until a cloud covered him. Then the disciples couldn't see him anymore.

Two angels appeared next to the disciples and said, "One day, Jesus will come back the same way you saw him go into heaven."

That means Jesus will one day come back to earth by floating down from the sky.

Then the angels left.

The disciples stayed in Jerusalem, just like Jesus had told them to do.

About 10 days after Jesus went back to heaven, the apostles sat in a house together. Suddenly, they heard a really loud rushing sound. It sounded like the worst storm they'd ever heard. But, amazingly, there was no wind. Only the sound of one.

As the sound rushed and roared, small flames of fire appeared and rested on each disciple. But nobody got burned.

Surely the disciples wondered aloud, "What in the world is going on?"

The funny thing was, each disciple spoke in a different language, a language they had never spoken before!

That was God's plan too! Isn't God cool like that? He always has a plan. He has the best plans ever.

As the tiny flames sat on the disciples, the Holy Spirit filled their hearts. This is the wonderful helper Jesus had promised to send.

It just so happened that a lot of Jewish people from many countries were in Jerusalem. All those visitors spoke their own languages.

The apostles hurried outside and started telling the crowd what had just happened.

Because each disciple spoke in a different language, all the different visitors could understand them.

Peter told the people about Jesus. He said, "God sent Jesus, the Savior, to earth to save the whole world. God raised Jesus back to life, and we've all seen him. Jesus is alive! Jesus rose into heaven and now sits at the right hand of God."

Peter talked some more.

The people listened.

And everyone heard in their own language.

People from many nations wanted to know how they could have salvation too. They wanted the Holy Spirit to live in their hearts.

Peter said, "Turn away from your sins and leave them behind you. Ask for forgiveness in the name of Jesus and be baptized. Believe that Jesus is God's Son. Accept him as your Savior."

Peter told the crowd of people that God loved every one of them. He said, "God's message is for each person, from every country in the world."

On that day, 3000 more people believed in Jesus.

Each day after that, the believers met together to learn more about Jesus. They shared everything they had with each other and ate meals together. They worshipped, prayed, and praised God.

More and more people came to know Jesus. The news about Jesus started spreading around the world.

All of this was part of God's great plan.

Reflection

- God loved the people too much to leave them alone, and Jesus was no longer there to guide them.

- God sent his Spirit, the Holy Spirit, to live in the hearts of those who believe that Jesus is God's Son and accept Jesus as their Savior.

- The Holy Spirit guides us, and the Holy Spirit helps us to tell people about God.

- Who can you tell about God tomorrow?

Prayer

Dear God, thank you for the amazing gift of your Holy Spirit! Thank you for a helper who lives inside my heart to guide me each day.

Thank you that the Holy Spirit helps me know right from wrong. Thank you that the Holy Spirit helps me know you better and shows me how to love you and others.

Thank you for loving me so much, God, that you are always with me. Amen.

Saul's Conversion

ACTS 9:1–31; 13:9

The disciples and new believers spoke boldly about Jesus. They told everybody they met about the Savior. Because of their boldness, many people believed that Jesus was God's Son. The people turned away from sin to live a good life. They treated their families with kindness. They helped their neighbors and friends. And they worshipped, prayed, and praised the Lord.

However, not everybody was happy about all these new believers. Many of the priests didn't like so many people talking about Jesus.

You're probably not surprised, right? After all, some of them were the same ones who'd wanted to get rid of Jesus!

One Jewish man named Saul wanted to put an end to the talk about Jesus. He wanted to get rid of the new believers.

Saul traveled north to the country of Syria. He'd heard that a bunch of new believers lived there. Saul had convinced the Jewish council to give him permission to arrest followers of Jesus in the city of Damascus.

But guess what God did before Saul could get there?

As Saul walked along, a bright light from heaven suddenly flashed around him, like lightning. The light was so bright that Saul fell to the ground and shut his eyes.

And as if that weren't enough to scare the sandals right off Saul's feet, guess what happened next?

Saul heard a voice.

"Saul, Saul, why do you want to hurt me? Why are you persecuting me?"

He still lay on the ground with his eyes shut. Saul had no idea who was speaking to him. "Who are you, Lord?" Saul asked.

"I am Jesus. The one you are persecuting." Jesus told Saul to get up, go into the city, and wait for instructions.

Saul had two big problems at that point.

Problem one: Most likely, Saul's knees were shaking so badly from fear that he had trouble standing up.

And problem two: The bright flash of light had taken away Saul's eyesight. Saul was blind.

The men traveling with Saul were just as terrified as Saul. They'd heard the conversation between Saul and Jesus, but they didn't see anyone but Saul.

The men led Saul into Damascus, where he spent the next three days neither eating nor drinking.

God spoke to a man named Ananias in a vision and told him to go visit Saul.

When Ananias heard Saul's name, he was afraid. "But, Lord," Ananias said, "I've heard about this man named Saul. He's harmed your holy people in Jerusalem, and now he wants to harm us."

Ananias must have been shaking in his sandals.

God said, "Saul is a new person. I chose Saul to tell the good news to the Gentiles."

Are you wondering what *gentiles* are? Back then, people who were not Jewish were called gentiles. Most gentiles lived in countries other than Israel.

Meanwhile, in the house where Saul was staying, Saul prayed. He was probably getting hungry by now, after not eating for three days, but food didn't seem very important to him at this time. Jesus was the most important thing to him, and he was afraid because he couldn't see.

While he prayed, Saul had a vision in his thoughts about a man coming to him to restore his sight.

And that's just what happened.

Ananias came to the door. Even though Ananias trusted God and obeyed, he must have been really nervous to meet Saul, the enemy of people who believed in Jesus.

But just like God had told Ananias, Saul was no longer the enemy of Jesus' people. Saul now loved Jesus as God's Son and wanted to be a follower too.

Ananias placed his hands on Saul. Right away, something like scales fell away from Saul's eyes.

"I can see," Saul announced. "I'm no longer blind!"

Saul traveled to Jerusalem to spend time with Jesus' disciples and learn about his Savior. Saul wanted to know every single detail so that he could tell others.

At first, the disciples didn't trust that Saul was really a changed man. But it didn't take them long to see the change in Saul's heart.

Saul had two names: Saul was his Hebrew name and Paul was his Roman name. He was so glad to be different now that from here on out, Saul only went by Paul.

From that time on, the Holy Spirit lived in Paul's heart. Paul spent the rest of his life traveling from nation to nation, telling the people about Jesus.

Reflection

- God used Saul, who had once bullied believers, to tell thousands of people about Jesus.

- We may sometimes think God can't use us because of some of the sins in our lives. But if God can use a man like Saul to change the world with the message of Jesus, then God can use us too.

- Do you have something big you want to do for God someday?

Prayer

Dear God, I'm sorry when I do things that hurt you. I'm sorry when I do things that hurt others. Please forgive me for those sins. Change my heart like you changed Saul's heart.

Help me want to tell everybody I meet about Jesus, just like Paul did.

Thank you for loving me. Amen.

Peter and Cornelius

ACTS 10

Long ago, God had asked Abram to leave his home and move to a new place. God had made a promise, or covenant, with Abraham. In God's promise, he said that Abraham would become the father of a great nation.

Remember, Abraham was like, "Whaaat? I don't even have one kid right now, and my wife and I are old."

Well, fast forward a bunch of years, and that's just what God did. Abraham's descendants—his children and their children and their children, and so on—were now a big nation, the Jewish people.

God had also promised Abraham that he would give the Promised Land, Canaan, to his chosen people. That had taken a lot of years, a lot of people's grumbling, some spies, and tons of manna and quail, but God had made that part of the covenant come true too. That Promised Land was now called the country of Israel.

If God says it, he'll do it!

God had said to Abraham, "And all peoples on earth will be blessed through you."

All people on earth were blessed through Abraham. Through his nation of Israel, God showed people of all countries how to live. And through Jesus, who had descended from Abraham, all peoples on earth could receive the forgiveness of sins and one day be in heaven with God.

God had done everything he'd promised.

His plan all along was for everybody to know him and to love him.

After Jesus rose to heaven and the Holy Spirit came into people's hearts, the disciples shared the good news about Jesus only with the Jewish people.

Here's what happened next.

A man named Cornelius was an officer in the Roman guard. Cornelius loved God. He also treated people kindly and helped people in need. His whole family loved and worshipped God. One afternoon, an angel appeared to Cornelius. The angel said, "God is pleased with your prayers and your gifts to the poor. Now, send some men to get Simon Peter and bring him here to talk with you."

Cornelius trusted God and obeyed. He sent three of his men to get Jesus' apostle Peter, even though Jewish people and non-Jewish people didn't hang out together back then.

Meanwhile, Peter had a vision. This was like a dream, but he was wide awake.

In his dream, a large sheet came down from heaven. The sheet contained all kinds of animals. It was like Noah's Ark on a sheet!

Peter heard a voice say to eat the animals.

Whaaat? thought Peter. He said, "I have never eaten anything unclean!" Peter knew the Jewish laws about what he could and could not eat.

Peter heard the voice again. This time, the voice said, "Do not call anything unclean that God has made clean."

Peter had the same vision, not once, or even twice. But three times. Then the dream ended.

While Peter was still thinking about the vision, the Holy Spirit told Peter, "Three men are outside looking for you. Do not be afraid to go with them, because I sent them."

The men told Peter about Cornelius's vision.

Peter may have thought, *I can't even figure out what my own vision means, and now you're telling me about your boss's vision!*

The next day, Peter traveled with the men to Cornelius's house. The house was full of people. Not Jewish people, though. Gentiles. They were Cornelius's relatives and friends. They wanted to hear about Jesus.

Peter realized that his vision from God meant he should tell everyone about God, not just Jewish people. He should even

eat meals with them, like friends do, even if they served food that Jewish people had once thought was "unclean."

As the people listened to Peter, he said, "I now know that God does not have favorites. God loves everyone, from every single nation in the world." Then Peter said, "The good news of Jesus is that anyone who accepts him as God's Son, and worships God, and does what is right, can receive forgiveness of their sins and be called a child of God."

At that moment, the Holy Spirit came upon all who believed.

The people were eager to know more about Jesus, so Peter stayed and taught them more.

Reflection

- God's plan to rescue the world through his Son, Jesus, began with the Jewish people. But God wanted everyone to come to know him.

- Jesus loves every single person in every part of the world. He wants all people on earth to hear the good news of Jesus.

- God doesn't have favorites. God loves everybody the same. And he wants us to love everybody as well.

- How can you show love to all people?

Prayer

Dear God, thank you for loving everybody in the whole world. Help me to show love and kindness to everybody too.

Help me want to tell everyone about Jesus. Amen.

Rhoda Helps Peter

ACTS 11:1–18; 12:1–17

At first, the other disciples didn't approve of Peter's time with Cornelius and his family.

"You ate with the gentiles?" someone asked Peter.

"That's not how we do things, Peter," another disciple might have said.

Peter wanted the others to know that God wanted everybody to hear the good news of Jesus.

"Let me start from the beginning," Peter said.

Apparently, Peter liked details. He liked telling the WHOLE story to everyone. Which is a good thing, because after Peter's WHOLE story of Jesus, Cornelius's WHOLE household became believers and followers of Jesus.

Peter told the disciples about his vision. And the sheet full of animals—Noah's Ark on a sheet. And the voice.

He told them the dream happened one, two, THREE times.

He told them about the three men showing up at his house. And Cornelius's vision.

That he and his friends had gone to Cornelius's house.

That he'd spoken to Cornelius and the family and a house full of people.

The whole household had believed in Jesus.

And the Holy Spirit had come into the hearts of the new believers.

Then Peter said, "If God gave them the same gift of the Holy Spirit that he gave all of us who believe in Jesus, who was I to think that I could stand in God's way?"

And the disciples said, "Okay, cool."

They might not have used those exact words, come to think of it. But they said something similar.

After Peter had spoken, the disciples realized that God wanted everyone to know about Jesus—Jews and Gentiles.

The disciples were so excited about the good news of Jesus, and their hearts were full of such joy, that they couldn't help but tell everyone they met about the Savior.

King Herod, however, didn't like the hubbub about this man named Jesus. Jealousy seeped into his heart, instead of joy.

King Herod told his guards to arrest Peter. So they put Peter in jail.

They chained Peter between two soldiers. Two other soldiers guarded the prison entrance.

"There's no chance this man will escape," King Herod might have sneered.

But King Herod didn't know Peter's God! And he didn't know that all of Peter's friends were praying for a miracle for Peter.

In the middle of the night, an angel appeared and a bright light filled the prison cell. The angel shook Peter and said, "Hurry, Peter! Get up!"

And just like that, the chains fell off Peter's arms!

The angel and Peter walked right past the first guard.

The angel and Peter walked right past the second guard.

When they came to the iron gate that led into the city, the gate opened by itself!

Peter suddenly realized he wasn't dreaming. He said, "The Lord sent an angel to rescue me!"

The angel vanished as quickly as he'd appeared. Peter hurried to the house of Mary, the mother of John, who was also called Mark, or John Mark. Peter knew his friends had been there all night long praying for him.

Peter knocked at the door.

A female servant named Rhoda came to the door. "Who's there?" she asked.

"It's me, Peter."

Rhoda got so excited when she heard Peter's voice that she didn't even open the door! She left Peter standing there and ran to tell everyone that Peter was outside.

Have you ever been so excited about something that you forgot about everything else? Or so excited that you could barely speak?

When Rhoda told the others, no one believed her! Maybe they thought she was dreaming.

Someone might have said, "Don't bother us now, Rhoda. We're praying for a miracle for Peter."

Rhoda insisted it was Peter, while Peter pounded on the door. Finally, someone opened the door. They were amazed to find that it really was Peter!

Peter told them the WHOLE story of his miraculous escape.

Peter was happy that his friends had prayed for him. He was thrilled that God had rescued him. And he was really glad a servant named Rhoda had helped him too.

Reflection

- Even though she was just a servant, Rhoda's prayers for Peter were important. God heard the prayers and saved Peter.

- God loves when we talk to him. He tells us that we can talk to him about anything! All our prayers are important.

- Where is your favorite place to pray?

- Why is that your favorite place to pray?

Prayer

Dear God, thank you for hearing all my prayers. Help me remember to talk to you when I'm scared or in trouble. Help me remember to thank you when everything is going well. Help me to always want to talk to you.

Please remind me to pray for others, especially when they're having a difficult time.

Thank you for listening, God. Thank you for the gift of prayer. Amen.

Paul Preaches and Writes Letters

ACTS 13–14; 16–28; ROMANS 10:9;
1 CORINTHIANS 13:4–8; GALATIANS 3:28;
EPHESIANS 2:4–9

From the moment Saul met Jesus on the road to Damascus, his heart filled with love and joy for his Savior. He spent the rest of his life as Paul, telling others about Jesus.

Over the years, Paul went on several journeys to preach. At many of the places he traveled, the people had never heard about Jesus. Paul shared the good news with the people he met and helped them to start churches.

A *church* wasn't always a building where people met to worship. Sometimes a church was simply a group of people who loved Jesus and wanted to serve him.

Paul told the people, "Because of God's great love for us, he sent his only Son, Jesus, to die on the cross for our sins. God's grace—his gift of love to us—saves us. Nothing more, nothing less. Salvation is a free gift to us when we believe in Jesus."

Paul told the people stories of Jesus' birth and life on earth. He told them about his death on the cross and his resurrection. Paul described how Jesus went back up to heaven. He described how God sent the Holy Spirit to live in believer's hearts, so that they could always be close to God.

He also said, "If you say with your mouth, 'Jesus is Lord,' and believe in your heart that God raised him from the dead, you will be saved. And you can live in heaven forever with God one day."

Paul loved Jesus so much that he just couldn't stop talking about him!

In one town, Paul preached for such a long time that it was way past midnight. He and the other people were in an upstairs room, three floors up. A young man named Eutychus wanted to hear every word. He sat in an open window, listening to Paul. He tried to stay awake, but his eyelids got heavier and heavier.

Eutychus couldn't help it—he fell asleep and tumbled right out the window. The young man fell down, down, down to the ground.

Paul ran downstairs and brought Eutychus back to life!

Have you ever fallen asleep in church? At least you didn't fall out of a window, right?

Sometimes another preacher or helper traveled with Paul, and they worked together to tell others about Jesus.

Most of Paul's travels were not easy ones. Three different times while Paul traveled by ship, terrible storms caused the ships to crash.

Many people were excited to hear the message of Jesus. But other people didn't want to listen. Some of the leaders got so angry with Paul that they had him arrested.

Paul became a prisoner in his own home. He was guarded and could no longer come and go as he pleased.

Do you think that stopped him from telling people about Jesus? Not at all!

Paul used his time in the house prison to write long letters to new believers and new churches, teaching them about Jesus.

In his letters, Paul reminded the people they were all equal in God's eyes. "God loves everyone the same," Paul wrote.

And he wrote a lot more.

"God doesn't have favorites between Jews and gentiles."

"God loves servants just as much as he loves important rulers and officers."

"God loves men and women the same too."

Paul made sure the people knew that, with Jesus, all people are equal.

As he wrote, Paul reminded believers to keep *running the good race*. Running the good race meant that following Jesus might be hard on some days, but they should keep following him anyway. Paul told them to never give up.

Paul wrote a lot about love in his letters too. He told the people that love is the greatest, most important thing. He wrote, "Love is patient. Love is kind. Love isn't jealous. Love isn't boastful or proud. Love isn't unkind to others. Love means thinking of others first, not yourself. Love forgives. Love protects and trusts. Love hopes for the best in others. And love lasts forever."

Paul let people know that God's love never ends.

Reflection

- When Paul met Jesus, his heart filled with such happiness that he couldn't wait to tell everybody about Jesus. His journeys to tell others weren't easy, but he still traveled all over.

- And when Paul couldn't travel, he wrote letters to keep telling people about Jesus.

- God wants us to tell others about Jesus too. Even when the journey is tough, God wants us to keep going.

- How can you tell people about God?

Prayer

Dear God, help me run the race of following Jesus every day. Bless me to have Paul's excitement for telling others about you.

And help me to love others because love is the greatest gift of all.

Thank you, God, for loving me. Amen.

John's Vision about a New Heaven and Earth

REVELATION 1; 4–5; 21–22

News about Jesus spread all over the world with the help of his apostles and other followers. Much like Paul, Jesus' apostle John enjoyed telling others about Jesus.

Roman leaders didn't want John telling people about Jesus. One of the Roman officials called for the arrest of John. Then he banished him to an island for prisoners, called Patmos.

One day, John had a vision that lasted a long time.

In the vision, John heard a voice as loud as a trumpet behind him. He turned and realized it was Jesus!

Right before John's eyes, he saw Jesus wearing a long robe with a golden sash. Jesus was glowing with brilliant light. So much light that his face looked bright as a sun, his hair looked as white as snow, and his eyes glowed like a blazing fire. His feet glowed too. This was the holy Son of God in all his glory.

What a magnificent sight that must have been for John, who'd been sent to a lonely prison far from home! To see Jesus face-to-face!

Jesus placed a hand on John and said, "Do not be afraid, John. I am the First and the Last. I am alive. I will live forever and ever."

Jesus had appeared to John to give him an important message. Jesus told John to write down his vision in a letter to send to churches in seven cities. He wanted the churches to know more about heaven. He wanted them to know what would happen in the future.

John's vision continued. In his vision, the door to heaven stood open. All at once, John went through the doorway, and then he was standing before a throne. God sat on the throne, and his radiance and glory shimmered in many colors. A dazzling rainbow surrounded the throne. It was shimmering too.

John saw a clear lake in front of the throne. Its water was as smooth as glass.

Four creatures were near the throne. Creatures like John had never seen before. One looked like a lion. Another resembled an ox. One creature had the face of a man. And the last creature looked like an eagle. Each of the creatures had six wings and lots of eyes.

The creatures spoke the same words over and over. They said, "Holy, holy, holy is the Lord God Almighty, who was, and is, and is to come."

Twenty-four elders wearing white robes and golden crowns sat around the throne. John saw the elders lay their crowns before the throne. And he heard them say, "You are worthy, our Lord and God, to receive glory and honor and power, for you created all things. By your will, all things were created and have their being."

Then John saw a lamb standing on the throne. He knew it was a symbol of the Lamb of God. It was Jesus. The lamb took a scroll from God's hand, opened it, and read from the scroll.

The scroll contained words about the future of the world. The scroll explained that Jesus will come back to earth one day. The old earth, full of sin and evil, will be destroyed. God will make a beautiful new heaven and earth.

John saw a vision of the Holy City—the new name for Jerusalem—coming down from the heavens. The Holy City shone with God's glory. It was made of pure gold, with high walls and 12 gates. A river as clear as crystal ran down the middle of the great street, which was also made of bright, beautiful gold. The tree of life, which had once stood in earth's Garden of Eden, was there, its branches full of leaves and fruit.

John learned that when Jesus returns, God will live among his people. God will make sure there is no more sin and no more evil. God will wipe away tears and take away sadness. No one will ever be sad again in that day. Every pain and ache and hurt will disappear.

Death will happen no more.

John heard God say from his throne, "I am making all things new. I am the *Alpha* and the *Omega*, which means the Beginning and the End."

John also heard God say that he will cast away all the evil people who didn't trust in God. The ones who didn't believe in Jesus will be banished from God forever.

Those with Jesus in their hearts will walk the streets of gold forever, in the presence of the holy and perfect God.

God loves his children—all his children—so much that he wants them to live with him forever.

Reflection

- What is your favorite Bible story about Jesus?

- One day, God will send Jesus back to earth. He'll take away sin and evil, pain and sadness and tears. The people who love God and have Jesus in their hearts will live with God in a new heaven.

- It will be a joyous time when we are able to live forever with God!

Prayer

Dear God, thank you for being the Beginning and the End. Thank you that you created the world a long time ago. Thank you that you'll one day come again so that we can live forever with you.

Thank you for loving me with an everlasting love and for sending Jesus to save the world so that I can live with you always.

I love you, God. Amen.

INDEX

ACKNOWLEDGMENTS

A special thanks to my husband, David. You're my biggest writing cheerleader, a wonderful husband and father, an amazing granddaddy, and my best friend forever. Thank you for taking such good care of our family!

To the four J's who made me a mommy—Jeremy, Jenifer, Jeb Daniel, and Jessica. Thank you for listening attentively to the Bible stories we read again and again, and for living out God's Word each day. You are so precious to me, and I love you more than I'll ever be able to express with words or actions. And to my son-in-love, Adam. Thank you for being a godly husband and daddy. I am so grateful God added you to our family!

To Benaiah (and other sweet Lavender grandchildren to come). Thank you for giving us the titles of Grandmommy and Granddaddy.

To my agent, Cyle Young, and his wife, Patty. Thank you for being the best agents ever!

To Penguin Random House. A huge thank you for the opportunity to join the PRH family. Words can never express the joy I have for this project! I'm thankful for each person who had a hand in making this book become a reality. You're amazing!

To those who've taught me to fall in love with God's Word—past, present, and future—I'm forever grateful.

Lastly, but first in my life, to my heavenly Father. *I've tasted and seen—YOU ARE GOOD!*

ABOUT THE AUTHOR

JULIE LAVENDER remembers hearing Bible stories ever since she was a little girl. Yet those stories have never grown old, as the Word of God is living and active.

She enjoyed immersing herself in God's Word to complete this book. It's her prayer that many—young children and adults who are young at heart—will fall more in love with God's Word and draw closer to him with each reading.

An author, journalist, and former homeschooling mom of 25 years, Julie holds a master's degree in early childhood education. She is married to her high-school and college sweetheart, and Julie and David are the parents of four, in-laws of one, and grandparents to a precious, almost-three-year-old grandson.

Julie loved living in various locations across the country as the wife of a United States Navy medical entomologist. She taught public school before becoming a stay-at-home, home-schooling mommy. After her husband retired from active duty, the Lavenders moved back to their hometown, and David began work as a wildlife biologist at a nearby army installation.

Julie's most recent book, *365 Ways to Love Your Child: Turning Little Moments into Lasting Memories*, encourages parents to show kids every day how much they are loved with simple but meaningful gestures and activities.

Julie loves to bake, travel, and spend time with her family.

Learn more about Julie at JulieLavenderWrites.com.

ABOUT THE ILLUSTRATOR

SHAHAR KOBER is an illustrator working from a very small studio, in a very small town, in a very small country. Over the years, Shahar has illustrated tens of books, but he also creates illustrations for newspapers, magazines, and animated films. He also teaches illustration. When Shahar doesn't illustrate, he enjoys the outdoors, taking care of his garden (which is very small as well!), and finding little insect friends there.

Learn more about Shahar at SKober.com.

Hi, parents and caregivers,

We hope you and your child enjoyed reading *Children's Bible Stories for Bedtime*. If you have any questions or concerns about this book, or have received a damaged copy, please contact **customerservice@penguinrandomhouse.com**. We're here and happy to help.

Also, please consider writing a review on your favorite retailer's website to let others know what you and your child thought of the book!

Sincerely,
The Zeitgeist Team